D0143393

To Harold "Bud" Clapp, friend
and Brother, who constantly
reminds me that in spite of all that
he has suffered, "it isn't the cross."

Table of Contents

Introduction 9

1. Staying Committed When Suffering Comes 13

2. When Bad Things Happen to Pretty Good People
Job 1 23

3. When Suffering Comes in Threes
Job 2:1-10 35

4. God's First Aid
Job 2:11-13 43

5. The Gift Nobody Wants
Job 3 51

6. Talks at the Dump: Round One
Job 4-14 61

7. Talks at the Dump: Round Two
Job 15-21 73

8. Talks at the Dump: Round Three
Job 22-31 85

9. What Friends Are For
Job 32-37 97

10. What Is God Saying to Us?
Job 38-41 111

11. After Suffering Come the Gifts
Job 42:1-6 121

12. Can We Live Happily Ever After?
Job 42:7-17 131

Conclusion 141

Bibliography 143

Introduction

Someone has said, "In life's loneliest spaces we most discover God." So much of life doesn't make sense to me. I don't understand why some women, who appear to be absolutely unqualified to love and nurture children, are able to bring them into the world with such ease. Names of married couples come to my mind at this very moment who have tried and tried unsuccessfully to have a single baby. I have cried with those moms and dads who have lost infants at birth. If pain can be measured by degrees their grief runs off the scale. I have wondered silently and aloud, "Where is God?"

On the days when I pick up our youngest daughter at school I find myself captivated by one mother who always comes in her blue Ford minivan. She is punctual and, like me, always parks in the same place. I love to watch her ritual. She climbs out of the van, walks to the front steps of the school building and waits. She never has to wait long. Soon a grade school age boy comes bouncing out the doorway, down the steps, and into his mother's arms. It is such a joyous occasion. I try not to miss it. That single hug between mom and son can transform my ordinary day into something extraordinary. It's when mom walks toward her van, hand in hand, with her little boy, that I notice the lines of anguish and concern on her face. Her sweet, precious, little child has Down's Syndrome. I know that these dear children are so loving and precious, yet, I can't help asking why? Where is God in that family?

If I take a brief moment to simply list some words that have invaded this place we call earth, the third planet from the sun, I think you will understand my own soul's wrestling. Consider these words.

Cancer. I know a mother who left three children and a husband behind when this disease took its final toll.

Suicide. My very first funeral was that of a young man in his early twenties who thought that life was not worth living. He hung himself.

War. I don't know if I can ever watch another network news program that brings Bosnia, Haiti, Somalia and Rwanda into my living room.

Where do I stop the list? Unemployment, homelessness, divorce, AIDS, floods, earthquakes, forest fires and the "catch-all," suffering. What I want to talk about in this book is not negative. Any of the experiences mentioned could sour one's view of life and of God. I'd like, however, to talk with you about a God who not only understands pain, but has experienced it Himself.

This God is never rushed or hurried by our agendas or needs. He is never late to the appointments with pain that each of us must keep. He always stands with us and beside us (Ps. 46:1ff). Our Father in heaven is never more present than in those seasons when our world seems to be falling apart.

Not long ago I was reminded of the penetrating and mysterious way in which God ministers to hurting people. It had been a long day and I had decided to take an afternoon walk. A very good friend and neighbor, Bud Clapp, was on my mind. As I strolled along I prayed for him and his family. Bud's wife, Lois, had battled with cancer for several years and recently endured a bone marrow transplant. She is a remarkable woman of courage and faith. When I do a quick inventory of all that the Clapps have endured I am awestruck at their perseverance. Bud has faced the daily challenges of a withered right arm since he was a boy. Their oldest son, Troy, had to have his right leg amputated when he was very young. They are an amazing family! I was talking with God about these wonderful people as I walked down the hill in front of their home. Bud came outside just as I "happened by." God's timing is astonishing! We talked and cried together as my friend revealed his honest pain and helplessness.

I'm not sure how much time had elapsed, but we had not gotten too far into our conversation when another neighbor, Kathy Judah, drove by and stopped. Her husband had been critically injured in an automobile accident several days prior and I asked her how their family was doing. Here I am standing between two hurting people, both of whom are uncertain as to the future of their loved one. In what could have been a very uncomfortable situation I found myself awestruck at how these two wounded people began to minister to each other. Before I knew it I was on the sidelines of the conversation watching and listening to God help in ways that I cannot put into words. Soon Kathy went on her way, Bud and I prayed together and I resumed my walk.

Several days later Kathy and her three children buried a husband and daddy. Several weeks later Bud preached his life partner's funeral. Lois died. That statement is a simple, two-word sentence packed to capacity with grief.

As far as I know there is only one person, just one, who is qualified to talk about what I want us to discuss in this book — God Himself. He believes that He has said everything that needs to be said and any other comments would be repetitive. If I could have a face to face chat with God I'd like to think that it would go something like this. God would remind me that I work for Him and that I had enough experience to be able to talk about the subject at hand if I wanted. I would convey to Him how unqualified I felt. I would remind Him that sometimes I feel like I'm just one of the guys sitting on the tailgate of a moving pickup truck. Now and then I think I know where the truck is headed and sometimes I am certain that I don't have the slightest clue where it's going. God, of course, would say He understands all my hesitation and doubt. I would respond, "Will the reader understand?" "Eventually," He would answer. "Are you sure?" I would wonder. "Absolutely," He would reply. So I go on pondering the way in which our Creator and Redeemer works in times of suffering and pain. One of the primary reasons I am writing this book is so that I might clarify my own confusion about God's presence in my times of distress. Of all the thousands of things that I do not understand about God I do believe and cling to this one fundamental truth. This God who is both transcendent and immanent is seldom early, but never late. "And so here I am, preaching and writing about things that are way over my head . . ." (*The Message*, Eph. 3:9).

CHAPTER ONE

Staying Committed When Suffering Comes

". . . I am happy because my happiness isn't based on happenings, but is based on Him, the Eternal."[1]

Life is hard.

I'm not sure when that thought first became a reality in my mind. I do know that the more I have read the book of Job the more I believe that life is tough. I love the opening line to this Old Testament story. "In the land of Uz there lived a man whose name was Job." That one line really doesn't tell us much of anything and yet it tells us so much. I do admit that more questions than answers surface in my thinking as a result of that initial sentence. Who is the author of this story? When was it written? Where is Uz? Most of what you or I can read about the background to Job will usually disclose that the author is unknown, the date uncertain, and the location obscure. No one really knows the whereabouts of Uz. It sounds like a place somewhere over the rainbow. Some folks even wonder whether this story is fabricated or true.

---

[1]E. Stanley Jones, *The Divine Yes* (Nashville: Abingdon, 1975), pp. 53-54. This was the last book that Jones wrote. It was written during a fourteen month period between a paralyzing stroke and his death. Though the book lacks some of the cohesiveness of his other writings it is a remarkable testimony to God's presence in times of suffering.

I have no problem believing it's genuine. Anybody who lives very long has no problem believing it either. The New Testament writers certainly treat Job as factual (James 5:11).

However, I admit that none of the above questions or notions have much importance for me. I don't mean to say that I am not interested in genuine study and exploration. I am. There is a peculiar trait, though, about pain and suffering. Hard times have a way of clearing away the "not-so-important stuff" from the essential and vital. I'm wagering that once we get into the heart and core of Job that most of us won't care much about who wrote it, and when, and where and how. I am writing primarily to fellow pilgrims and strugglers who, now and then, get bumped, bruised and battered on the road to the Celestial City.

If you have studied the Bible very long you know that many Old Testament characters have names that tell you lots about who they were and what they were like. Job's name can mean one of two things. It can mean "where is my father" or it can mean "no father." Now that interests me! Perhaps hiding behind the name of Job is a man who could have been an orphan ("Where is my father?") or an illegitimate son ("I have no father.") More questions surface. What kind of person was this Job? What was he like? Did he like kids? Did he love his wife? What was she like? Did Job take walks? Did he work hard? Did he have a favorite season? Did he keep a clean barn? Did he care for the widower who lived down the road in the small, white house? Did he ever give out any free advice? Did he ever have pain or suffering prior to what happens to him in the story that bears his name? Could he tell a good story, in the evening, out on the front porch, with the kids all around him? Could he paint visions of sugar plums dancing in the their heads? Did his wife always have jobs for him to do? Did he treat his employees with respect? What kind of life did he live? Was he nice? Was he polite? Did he have a name for his ranch? Was he a supporter of the

Chamber of Commerce of Uz? Did they have a sports team in town? Did he go see them compete? Did he live and die with how well the Uz "Zebras" had played in their previous outing? What was he really like? And more than anything did he love God and neighbor as he loved himself?

Of course, many of these questions are answered simply by reading the story of Job. What I would like to do in this chapter is identify and eliminate seven myths that surround the subject of suffering.

Myth #1. Good People Never Suffer.

Some people truly believe this lie. They have Bible passages to support their convictions. For example, Proverbs 12:21 is often used. "No harm befalls the righteous, but the wicked have their fill of trouble." It is important to remember that Proverbs are not intended to be exhaustive in application. They are sayings that enshrine and capture certain truths gleaned from general observation of daily life. The above proverb is generally true, but then there is Job. There is life's reality. Job is described as "blameless" and the author uses three other synonyms to complete the portrait of this man. We'll talk more about that in the next chapter. It does impress me that the Hebrew word for "blameless" depicts a person whose heart is completely sold out and in love with God. It doesn't mean that Job was sinless. It means that he was incredibly consistent in his walk with God. The word describes someone who is innocent and full of integrity. Job's life modeled what we would call "the straight life." This rancher from Uz exemplifies clean living at its very best. People didn't come any better than Job.

If you'll jump ahead to Job 6:21 you'll notice that even after all the suffering this godly man is still able to say, "Teach me, and I will be quiet; show me where I have been wrong." Good people do suffer.

15

Myth #2. Bad Guys Always Suffer.

Before we get too far along in our study and reflection we are going to meet three of Job's very best friends. They believe this myth with all their hearts. "If you're suffering," they will tell Job in various ways, "you've done something terribly wrong. Admit it!" Check out chapter four. One of Job's companions, Eliphaz by name, has come to comfort this suffering man. This is his advice.

"Consider this: Who, being innocent, has ever perished? Where were the upright ever destroyed? As I have observed, those who plan evil and those who sow trouble reap it" (Job 4:7).

Now there is a partial truth in Eliphaz's statement. We do reap what we sow (Gal 6:7). But Job sees so many wicked things going on around him. He observes the rebellious living without worry and concern. Here he is trying to live for the Lord and he can hardly get through the day. Sound familiar? Remember Jesus' words, Luke 6:35, "God is kind to the ungrateful and wicked." Sometimes bad guys don't suffer. Sometimes they live in the lap of luxury. My grandmother would have put it this way. "Sometimes folks live pretty high on the hog, but the hog doesn't last forever."

Myth #3. Only Sin Causes Suffering.

Here is another myth we are going to hear Job's friends pass along to him. They mean well. Notice Job 22:5. Listen for a moment to the accusations Job's buddies make. ". . . Are not your sins endless? You demanded security from your brothers for no reason; you stripped men of their clothing, leaving them naked. You gave no water to the weary and you withheld food from the hungry. . . ." Verses nine and ten enlarge the list. ". . . You sent widows away empty-handed. . . . That is why snares are all around you."

16

Ouch! Talk about kicking a man when he is down. It is true that sin does cause suffering. No question about that. However, sin is not the only cause of suffering. Sometimes we suffer because we live in a fallen world, a world marred with the pain of man's blunder in Eden. Sometimes we suffer because we make bad choices. The theology of Job's three friends could not admit to these other possibilities. That is more contemporary than we would like to admit.

I've been recalling a number of books that I read several years ago when I was first exploring Job. Rabbi Harold Kushner's work, *When Bad Things Happen To Good People*, was one of those books. The second chapter of that book is devoted to Job. Listen to Kushner's perspective of Job's debate with his three friends.

> "Are you implying that my children were wicked, and that is why they died? Are you saying that I am wicked, and that is why all this is happening to me? Where was I so terrible? What did I do that was so much worse than anything you did . . . ?" The dialogue becomes heated, even angry. The friends say: "Job, you really had us fooled. You gave us the impression that you were as pious and religious as we are. But now we see how you throw religion overboard the first time something unpleasant happens to you. You are proud, arrogant, impatient, and blasphemous. No wonder God is doing this to you. It just proves our point that human beings can be fooled as to who is a saint and who is a sinner, but you can't fool God."[2]

How would you like those guys to visit your hospital bed? Sometimes suffering can't be explained at all.

------

[2]Harold Kushner, *When Bad Things Happen To Good People* (New York: Avon Books, 1981), p. 34. This is a splendid book that deals with the reality of suffering in this world. Though Kushner writes from a deist's viewpoint his insights are invaluable.

Myth #4. Trust God And Suffering Will Vanish.

That sounds plausible. It parallels what the unholy trinity of friends tell Job when he's flat on his back. But this myth doesn't square with the rest of Scripture. Stroll over to 2 Corinthians 12 and take a look at verses seven to nine. Paul is talking about some of his own suffering. "To keep me from becoming conceited because of these surpassing great revelations, there was given me a thorn in my flesh, a messenger of Satan, to torment me. Three times I pleaded with the Lord to take it away from me. But He said to me, 'My grace is sufficient for you, for my power is made perfect in weakness.'" Paul trusted God with all his heart. It didn't change his suffering. It only changed his attitude.

Myth #5. If God Cared Suffering Would Vanish.

Without saying too much too soon we are going to chew on this myth throughout the book. I honestly believe it would be a breeze for God to step in and stop suffering. That is the kernel of truth in this myth. Our Father in heaven could make Rin-Tin-Tin, the Navy Seals, and Dirty Harry look foolish. Instead, our Lord walks beside us. Job couldn't see that. I don't see it sometimes either. Maybe you don't. But God does care. C.S. Lewis understood that. In his classic book, *The Problem of Pain,* he wrote:

> We want not so much a father in heaven as a grandfather in heaven whose plan for the universe was such that it might be said at the end of the day, "A good time was had by all. . . ." I should very much like to live in a universe which was governed on such lines, but since it is abundantly clear that I don't, and since I have reason to believe nevertheless that God is love, I conclude that my conception of love needs correction . . . .[3]

---

[3]C.S. Lewis, *The Problem of Pain* (New York: MacMillan, 1962), p. 40. In order to have a greater appreciation of this work and *A Grief Observed* I recommend that you rent the video, *Shadowlands.*

Myth #6. Work Hard And Suffering Will Vanish.

You've heard that one, haven't you? Just buckle down, suck it up, and everything will turn out rosy. Eliphaz, one of the three friends, was hinting at this myth in chapter four, when he spoke to Job. "Think how you have instructed many, how you have strengthened feeble hands. Your words have supported those who stumbled (In Hebrew that phrase implies: "You've kept them on their feet with your words."); you have strengthened faltering knees. But now trouble comes to you and you are discouraged; it strikes you, and you are dismayed." Do you hear, Eliphaz? "Bear down, Job!" "Get with it!" "You're not trying hard enough!" "You're not practicing what you preach!" Do you see the myth? There is no question that some folks never try to get through their suffering. They wallow in it, loving the attention, but sometimes even hard work won't squeeze the pain out of suffering.

Myth #7. No One Understands My Suffering.

Maybe this is the most treacherous myth of all. Job slides right into this one himself. He doesn't need any help with this lie. You really can't blame him. Who hasn't been there? Stuck in the mire of self-pity. That's what is so powerful about this deception. We see ourselves in Job's yielding to the myth. Turn to chapter 29 of Job. His last words are recorded there. From verse seven on to the end of the chapter Job talks about what once was, how people used to show him respect (29:8,9), how everyone waited to hear what he had to say (29:10). He talks about all the things he once did (29:12ff). Finally Job declares, "I dwelt as a king among his troops; I was like one who comforts mourners" (29:25). This man of sorrow knew the "high-life," but all that changed. In 31:35 Job cries out, "Oh, that I had someone to hear me!" There it is. No one understands my suffering. And what happens after that? Well, we will save it for later.

19

It is difficult to look pain squarely in the face. There are so many unanswered pieces. What is it like to suffer? Sometimes people get together and they'll share their pain and after hearing enough of those stories I've come to believe that suffering is suffering. It's like sin in some way. Sin is sin. To steal a candy bar from the local grocery is the same as cold-blooded murder in a back alley. I think suffering is like that. The degrees are something we put on it, not God. I believe God hurts with us just as much over cancer, or divorce, or death, as He does over stress, or a broken arm, or criticism. Pain has no levels. The heart can't tell the difference between a cruel word or a fractured leg. It simply knows it hurts.

A little girl came home from school one day. She looked as if someone had done something terrible to her, something one person can't totally explain to another person. Her daddy met her at the screen door, between the washroom and the garage. When she saw him she burst into tears. They were tears like lemon drops, large, wet, sad tears. Tears that spring up from something that is broken inside, like a busted water main. This father and daughter sat down on the little step that rests beneath the screen door. He held her like he did when she was a baby. He asked her with his eyes and with his arms what had happened and out it came. "Daddy, I don't think anybody loves me." Have you ever felt like that?

Pain sometimes comes as an announcement around the supper table or in the kitchen. Someone will say, "I went to the doctor today and the tests were positive." Or the announcement will come over the phone. "Could you come to the hospital?" Or someone will say, "We don't know where he is," or "It happened at 3:00 this morning. Could you come over, please?" The subject matter in Job is suffering. It is not a complex analysis. There are no detailed reports. There are no profound answers offered as to why we suffer. Suffering is simply told as a story and everyone who reads it is invited to see their own story within its pages.

I want to let you in on a secret. A number of years ago I was the preacher of a certain congregation. In the first year there I felt as if I had stepped into the "Twilight Zone." The first Sunday I preached a man came up to me. I'll never forget his words: "You're not a biblical preacher. You don't preach from the Bible. I'll not be back." It stung like a hornet. I came to realize later that what he meant was I didn't preach on his favorite themes. But I want you to know that I harbored what he said in my heart.

Not long after that episode a woman in that church told me, "You're not filled with the Spirit." And I harbored that too. I heard other ripples of unrest from several folks. I confronted it when I felt I should, but the criticisms continued. Finally there was a meeting between myself, the associate minister, one of the elders and this person who continued to complain. We met in her living room and all the accusations and criticisms came out. Poison filled the room. "You aren't a good teacher." "You don't let the Spirit lead enough." "You're trying to drive us out of the church." "You're too immature to lead this congregation." I responded with both barrels! Even that didn't soothe the pain. The woman and her family left the church and eventually moved away. And I harbored everything they had said.

I received anonymous letters as well. One individual asked me if I was trying to destroy their church. I harbored that one too. All kinds of little bickerings and squabbles continued to surface. I got those inevitable phone calls. I started feeling sorry for myself. "No one understands my suffering," I would mutter to myself. My preaching suffered. I became suspicious. I decided I'd keep to myself and look for another place to serve. I was told, "You laugh too much." "You're too serious." I buried it all deep within my inner being. My wife and I left town and went to St. Louis for a convention. A couple of people from the church met us for lunch. I was so discouraged, I'm sure it was obvious. I'll never forget what that dear brother in Christ said to me. He looked right at me and said, "You're riding loose in the saddle. You've got to decide whether or not you want to stay on. God called you here. He's not done. Are you?" I decided I wasn't. I began to forgive and ask to be forgiven. It didn't happen overnight, but God began to do a good work in that church and in me.

The greatest mystery in Job is not the problem of suffering and why it happens. The greatest mystery is faith and grace blooming out of suffering and pain. To love life, but hold it loosely; to experience hurt at the hands of mean-spirited people, but still forgive; to look into the eyes of God and see that He's not to blame; all of that is the greatest mystery! If you long to experience that kind of freedom then you must embrace this God who is seldom early, but never late.

CHAPTER TWO

When Bad Things Happen to Pretty Good People
Job 1

"I was talking to a bishop who had retired. . . . He was frustrated and told me so. . . .When the outer strands were broken by retirement, the inner strands were not enough to hold him. . . . Fortunately, with me, surrender to Jesus was the primary thing, and when the outer strands were cut by this stroke, my life didn't shake."[1]

I remember the day as if it happened this morning. It was a beautiful summer day. I think it was 1961. A bunch of kids, including me, were down at the Edde house, because their granddaughter, Christie Roy, had come in from the country to spend the day at her grandparents. Christie can only be described as sweet. It was easy to be her friend. For all the kids along Sullivan Street Mr. and Mrs. Edde were adopted grandparents. No one else in our neighborhood let children play in their yard and run through their hedges and climb their trees and eat cookies and sit on their front porch. Bruce MacClaren's dad used to yell at us and tell us to go play somewhere else. Old Bill George didn't like us around his place. The Leeper sisters, who lived across from the parsonage where I grew up, were nice enough elderly widows, but they couldn't hear anything and there wasn't anything worth exploring around their house. There was that old outhouse in their backyard that their brother, the

---

[1] Jones, *The Divine Yes*, p. 63.

23

president of the Farmer's Bank, had nailed shut. Of course, anything nailed shut must be worth investigating. So, on occasion, we would try opening it and he would keep nailing it shut. It was a "need" relationship. It wouldn't have been any fun if Mr. Leeper had not continued to put up more nails and boards. He needed us to keep his life from absolute boredom and we needed him to teach us the importance of perseverance. "If at first you don't succeed, try, try again." Who knew what might be inside that old outhouse. There were grapevines that had grown up all around it. Perfect soil, I guess, for growing grapes. We use to imagine what was inside that ancient bathroom. Maybe a skeleton, the remains of a treasure hunter who had been mining for gold or silver and he accidently had gotten locked inside and never got out. Perhaps there was money inside, from Mr. Leeper's bank, cash that he had secretly hidden away, thinking no one would ever look for embezzled loot in an outhouse.

On this day we were down at the Edde's playing with Christie, doing what kids do on summer days. Hide-n-Seek. Mother-May-I. Simon Says. Some of us were playing jacks on the front porch. It was one of those enchanted days. If someone blindfolded you and you couldn't see the green leaves in the tree or the clear sky, or the flowers alongside the house, you might think it was Spring or Indian summer. It was so pleasant, a fun day, not much fighting or arguing over who got caught in Hide-n-Seek. What made it memorable, though, was none of those things. Those kind of memories get lost in the clutter of our minds. It takes something unusual to jolt our recollections. For some reason — maybe there doesn't even have to be a reason — we were playing beside the big oak tree that set alongside the gravel driveway. That magnificent tree set on a little hill and its trunk sloped downward toward the driveway like a playground slide. It was slick, worn down by all of us playing on it. Grandpa Edde had often meant to put some cement around those slippery, exposed roots, in order to make it safer.

Christie's mom had gotten into her car and double checked to make sure everyone was out of the way. I was standing on the little hill on the opposite side of the driveway, in Bruce MacClaren's yard. Christie was at the foot of that tree, beside the driveway. My memory does not recall all that followed. I do recall how everything seemed to go into slow motion. The car backed up. Christie slipped. Terrible screaming rang out. Grandpa Edde ran to the back of the car. Mrs. Roy stopped the car. There was Christie, underneath the automobile, both of her legs crushed. I couldn't look at her. Even as I write these words I find myself beginning to cry over her pain. I don't remember much of what happened next. The day ended for all of us kids. Christie lived. She had a long and terrible recovery. I think her mother had a long journey as well. My friend walked again, first with crutches and braces, finally on her own. Eventually my family moved away. My Dad followed the calling voice of God to another congregation. I do remember going out to Christie's house before we left. Maybe a year or so after the accident. She looked a lot older to me. More than a year's worth of old. Perhaps that was the first time I began to ask questions about bad things happening to good people.

Harold Kushner might be correct.

There is only one question which really matters: why do bad things happen to good people? All other theological conversation is intellectually diverting; somewhat like doing the crossword puzzle in the Sunday paper and feeling very satisfied when you have made the words fit; but ultimately without the capacity to reach people where they really care. Virtually every meaningful conversation I have ever had with people on the subject of God . . . has either started with this question, or gotten around to it before long.[2]

---

[2]Kushner, *When Bad Things Happen To Good People*, p. 6.

If anything is true about Job it is the fact that it is filled with questions. The tough part is that most of us don't have answers. I do want to further introduce you to the three chief characters in the story.

The first character is obviously Job. I'll call him Job, the good. Job 1:1-5 gives us this description.

> In the land of Uz there lived a man whose name was Job. This man was blameless and upright; he feared God and shunned evil. He had seven sons and three daughters, and he owned seven thousand sheep, three thousand camels, five hundred yoke of oxen and five hundred donkeys, and had a large number of servants. He was the greatest man among all the people of the East. His sons used to take turns holding feasts in their homes, and they would invite their three sisters to eat and drink with them. When a period of feasting had run its course, Job would send and have them purified. Early in the morning he would sacrifice a burnt offering for each of them, thinking, "Perhaps my children have sinned and cursed God in their hearts." This was Job's regular custom.

There are six brief characteristics that describe Job, the good. The first four descriptive traits are explicit in the Scriptures.

1. He was blameless.

Remember that the word for blameless describes someone who is innocent, full of integrity, modeling the straight life. The characteristic here does not imply absolute sinlessness. It reveals a consistency of moral soundness.

2. He was upright.

This simply means that Job was completely honest, particularly in his business dealings. The word "upright" can mean "straight" in Hebrew. It's the notion of not deviating from what God has set as a standard.

3. He was a man who feared God.

Job was a man who was totally aware of God. There was a genuine reverence in his relationship with his Creator. This man from Uz submitted to God's majesty as he saw and understood it.

4. He shunned evil.

Job hated and rejected whatever was in contrast to what he believed God to be. He rejected anything that appeared wrong. Notice that Job isn't portrayed as making a big deal about any of this. He's not boastful. He's not a self-righteous Ricky. Job isn't a braggart. He is portrayed as choosing a path of righteousness for his life and he sticks to it. There is a fifth trait that is implied in this paragraph of Scripture, especially verses two and three.

5. He is blessed by God.

Look at all the numbers mentioned. Seven sons, three daughters, 7,000 sheep, 3,000 camels, 500 yoke of oxen, 500 donkeys. All of these numbers in Hebrew symbolize completeness, the ideal, or perfection. It is a picture of abundance, a godly view of the rich and famous.

6. He is the spiritual leader of his family.

Job is pictured as concerned for their spiritual welfare. He is deeply committed to the godliness of his own family. He is like an Ozzie Nelson, a Robert Young in "Father Knows Best," or a Dr. Huxtable. This family has a dad who cares about their relationship with God.

The summary statement in verse three, "the greatest man among all the people of the East," leaves us with the impression that Job was a living legend in his own time. How he handles abundance says so much about him. How he handles complete destruction says even more! Job was simply a good man.

The second character at the outset of the story is Satan. I'll simply identify him as Satan, the bad. Read on (1:6-12).

> One day the angels came to present themselves before the Lord, and Satan also came with them. The Lord said to Satan, "Where have you come from?" Satan answered the Lord, "From roaming through the earth and going back and forth in it." Then the Lord said to Satan, "Have you considered my servant Job? There is no one on earth like him; he is blameless and upright, a man who fears God and shuns evil" (note the repetition with 1:1). "Does Job fear God for nothing?" Satan replied. "Have you not put a hedge around him and his household and everything he has? You have blessed the work of his hands, so that his flocks and herds are spread through the land. But stretch out your hand and strike everything he has, and he will surely curse you to your face." The Lord said to Satan, "Very well, then, everything he has is in your hands, but on the man himself do not lay a finger." Then Satan went out from the presence of the Lord.

Three things stand out about Satan.

1. He is cynical.

What God is enthusiastic about Satan views sourly. The devil's name in Hebrew has an article in front of it. The Scripture literally reads in verse six "the Satan also came with them." His name means "adversary" or "opposer." It can even mean "accuser." Satan is sarcastic and negative. Whatever God is for he opposes. The Creator of heaven and earth is for this good man Job, but the archenemy is seeking out his prey.

2. He is abusive.

The devil's language and attitude reek of verbal abuse. He is curt, sharp and negative. "Does Job fear God for nothing?"

(vs. 9) Can you hear what the deceiver is saying about God? "Job worships you for only selfish reasons, to get what he wants. Strip away everything he has and he'll drop you like a hot potato. Take away the good times and Job will crumble." Satan's words tear down and never build up.

3. He is arrogant.

The portrait of Satan here drips with pride. I think it's one of the ugliest pictures in the Bible. He's "struttin' his stuff" as if he owns the whole world. There is a parallel to this picture over in 1 Peter 5:8. "The devil prowls around like a roaring lion looking for someone to devour." His arrogance has no bounds. He is not some comical character. He doesn't wear red tights. He has no pointed tail, horns on his head and a pitchfork in his hand. The Opposer is cynical, abusive and arrogant.

C.S. Lovett, in his practical little book, *Dealing With the Devil*, offers these four helpful suggestions about our enemy.

> First, have a healthy respect for our adversary.
> Second, know how he operates.
> Third, have a defense system for protecting your thought life.
> Fourth, be equipped with the spiritual mechanics for resisting him.[3]

Hang on to this picture of Satan. There is a third character I want us to meet. He is the hero of every narrative. God, Himself, enters the story. I'll call him "The One who knows." The writer of Job makes precise and vivid strokes in his painting of God.

1. He is sovereign.

Nothing happens that is not under His control. In Job 1:6 every angel comes before God to present himself. In the

---

[3]C.S. Lovett, *Dealing With the Devil* (Baldwin Park, CA: Personal Christianity, 1967), p. 13.

Hebrew Bible the verse literally reads, "They stationed themselves before Him." God is portrayed as paying attention to all that occurs. He is Lord of all creation. What is so amazing is that this Supreme Ruler allows that which He has created to question Him. God is not threatened by interrogation or rebellion.

2. He is loving.

He puts no false walls around all that is rightfully His. He is patient, kind, not envious, not boastful, not proud, not rude, not self-seeking, and not easily angered. Satan seems to particularly delight in attacking God's love.

3. He is proud of His children.

Take another look at 1:8. God says to Satan, "Have you considered my servant Job?" I deeply appreciate how one commentator put it.

> Note that it is God, not the Satan, who calls attention to the exemplary life of Job. Like a proud parent, God shows off Job to the Satan, as though to challenge his cynical estimate of the best in human nature.[4]

I want us to see how all of this is presented. Job, the good, is seen in an ideal setting, like a three day trip to Disneyworld. In contrast God and Satan are in direct conflict. Why? Any quick response to that question would be premature. The story moves so rapidly from this point on we can hardly keep pace. Because everything we build upon in our study depends on our view of chapter one I don't want us to miss any of the details. Read on.

---

[4]Victor E. Reichert, *Job*. Edited by A. Cohen. (London: The Soncino Press, 1974 reprint), p. 3. This very fine Jewish commentary offers valuable insight into Hebrew interpretation and thought.

One day when Job's sons and daughters were feasting and drinking wine at the oldest brother's house, a messenger came to him and said, "The oxen were plowing and the donkeys were grazing nearby, and the Sabeans attacked and carried them off. They put the servants to the sword, and I am the only one who has escaped to tell you!" While he was still speaking, another messenger came and said, "The fire of God fell from the sky and burned up the sheep and the servants, and I am the only one who has escaped to tell you!" While he was still speaking, another messenger came and said, "The Chaldeans formed three raiding parties and swept down on your camels and carried them off. They put the servants to the sword, and I am the only one who has escaped to tell you!" While he was still speaking, yet another messenger came and said, "Your sons and daughters were feasting and drinking wine at the oldest brother's house, when suddenly a mighty wind swept in from the desert and struck the four corners of the house. It collapsed on them and they are dead, and I am the only one who has escaped to tell you!" (Job 1:13-19)

The unimaginable becomes reality. Robbery and murder enter. Cattle and camels exit. Lightning and tornado enter. Sheep and children exit. The good, the bad and the One who knows all, combine to usher in this drama of dramas. The story moves so rapidly from Eden to nightmare. It leaves us breathless. We wonder and question and probe. All we find is confusion.

I want to set the stage so that we can really hear Job. Perhaps the best way to do that is admit that I have as many questions as you do. It is not just, why do bad things happen to good people? There are other questions as well.

What is Satan doing in heaven?
Why does God speak with the Accuser?
Does God take bets on His people?
Does He play a part in human suffering?
Why doesn't He just say, "No," to this challenge posed by Satan?

31

Suffering births questions. When pain enters our world, whether it is happening to me directly or I am simply studying the subject, real, deep, soul-searching questions surface.

When I was serving in the local church I spent a lot of time in the hospital. Even now I find myself visiting and listening to students or colleagues who find themselves in need of a physician's care. People always have questions at the hospital. I've been asked a hundred different ones.

Does my wife know?
Am I going to die?
What time is it?
Can I know I am saved?
I'm scared. Can you help me?
Why is this happening to me?
How bad is it?
Will you tell the children?
How much time do I have?

Why do bad things happen to good people? I don't know. I do believe there are a few things that can help each of us when faced with overwhelming questions.

1. Look to God.

That's what Job did. "At this, Job got up and tore his robe and shaved his head. Then he fell to the ground in worship" (1:20).

When things turned sour and all hell broke loose, Job fell on his knees and looked to God. I believe with all my heart that nothing happens in this world that escapes the attention of my heavenly Father. His great longing for me is that I become Christlike. Even Jesus did not escape the suffering of this world. How could I think I might be exempted? While on the cross of Golgotha Jesus looked to the Father.

32

2. Look inside.

Job 1:21 says, "Naked I came from my mother's womb, and naked I will depart." The agonizing man from Uz captured something in that one sentence! When we look inside of ourselves, really look, honestly look, we know we came with nothing and we leave nothing. When suffering strips us down to the "nubbies" we really have the potential to receive 20-20 vision.

3. Look beyond.

The very next line in 1:21 reads, "The Lord gave and the Lord has taken away; may the name of the Lord be praised." Rather than surrender to remorse and bitterness Job seems filled with hope. God has something better ahead. "In all of this, Job did not sin by charging God with wrongdoing" (1:22).

An imaginary story is circling in my mind. It seems so far away and so long ago. There was a man named Bert Clesson. He lived in an old blue and white trailer at the edge of town. Most people thought Bert was odd. I suppose they thought they had good reason for their conclusions, because he always smiled, never really speaking to anyone. People would see Bert moving his lips, as if talking to himself, as he chugged along through the alleyway behind their houses. Rumors abounded as to why Bert was the way he was. Someone said, "Bert was injured in an automobile accident while coming home from church one summer evening. He was never the same after that." Most folks agreed that there was no one more faithful than Bert. The few who still spoke with the old man said he was still mentally sharp. It simply took him longer to express it now. He was a friend to all, even if everyone was not a friend to him. Mr. Clesson had a regular routine of visiting the trash bins and barrels behind all the business establishments. He would throw the stuff he found into a little red wagon that he pulled along as he went from place to place. He would gather enough of these "treasures" and haul them down to the local salvage yard and collect what ever he could.

Many of the children played out what they heard their parents say behind closed doors. When Bert would come along the children would taunt him. "Bert," they would say, "Did your mother have any kids that lived?" "Bert, if you put your brains in a glass of water it would look like a duck on Lake Erie."

The children would recite poetry.

> Roses are red,
> Violets are blue.
> Bert is so dumb,
> He belongs in the zoo!

Bert would just smile and carry on with his appointed rounds. The people of the town found him one Saturday morning sitting in his chair, looking out the window of his blue and white trailer. He was dead. They discovered a will neatly folded and legally documented in a little box beside the sink. Bert had managed to save 80,000 dollars. It was all bequeathed to the community he loved. One simple line told the whole story. In scribbles barely legible, Bert wrote, "I don't know why all this happened to me, but when bad things happen to people only God matters."

When we know we are loved by God what else is there? He is seldom early, but never late. Praise Him, He is never late!

CHAPTER THREE
When Suffering Comes In Threes
Job 2:1-10

"As I look at the Bible, the evidence seems inconclusive. Sometimes God causes suffering for a specific reason – usually as a warning. Sometimes Satan caused it. In other cases, such as the Siloam disaster Jesus discusses, God wasn't intending any specific message. But one passage about suffering in the Bible – the most exhaustive treatment of the topic – has an unmistakable message. It comes in the Book of Job, smack in the middle of the Old Testament."[1]

I hated to wear boots to school. As long as I can remember I despised those black, rubbery things that slipped on over my shoes and buckled in the front. I believed they served no useful purpose in a boy's life. They were ugly and cumbersome and a bother to get on and off, simply a mega pain. The only time I believed they served mankind was when I imagined myself to be Sgt. Saunders, Cage, Kirby or Little John from the T.V. show, *Combat.* Then you needed boots in order to wade through the mud and water of hostile enemy territory down by the local creek. I would hum the theme song from the show as I snuck through enemy occupied territory. No one on a secret mission, behind German lines, ever took off without his boots.

---

[1]Phil Yancey, *Where Is God When It Hurts* (Grand Rapids: Zondervan, 1977), p. 67. Yancey writes an extraordinarily inspirational book that deals concretely and realistically with the problem of pain.

I still recall, however, my mother's voice of reality as I would leave the house for school on a snowy day. "Johnny," she would say, "Don't forget your boots!" There was no negotiation or compromise. As far as mom was concerned no one was fully or properly dressed without boots. As I got older I thought I got smarter. I would wear those boots when I went out the back door, but I had a secret place alongside the house, behind the fir trees where I would take off the boots and dance off to school bootless.

All dishonorable things catch up with us eventually. I got sick. Mom had found out I hadn't been wearing my boots through the cold, wet days of winter. So when I came up ill you would expect I would hear those famous words, "I told you so," but I never heard them. Mom did what she did best. She took care of me. I missed school. I missed my favorite class, Art with Mr. Ryan. He made the subject fun. A few days went by and I started to feel better, so I asked my mother if I could go to school in the afternoon. I didn't want to miss Art again. Of course, I was still sick, but wouldn't admit it. That was a mistake and ushered in a series of awful events.

Sometimes bad things do come in threes. First, I felt worse as the day wore on and should have stayed in bed. Second, when I got to school Mr. Ryan was sick. No Art class. Third, Mrs. Perry, the Social Studies teacher, would teach an extra section of her favorite subject, not mine. She yelled at me for not knowing the capital of Chile. I said it was Buenos Aires. Mrs. Perry loudly corrected me. "It's Santiago!" "Why aren't you more like your sister, Janie?" she asked. I felt terminally ill. I hated boots even more!

How does a person deal with bad things that come in bunches? My old Homiletics professor used to say, "They come in threes." He wasn't superstitious. He was simply commenting on his many experiences and observations. So what do I do when bad things surround me like hungry hyenas? In this incredible story of suffering Job was hit by three terrible blows.

1. *Job lost his wealth.*

Everything! Everything that bore his name, he lost. His livestock, his crops, his land, his servants, his home, his money, even his kids. Ten fresh graves reminded Job, every day, of his loss. I can't imagine losing one of my children, let alone losing ten. Let that sink in. As this righteous man looked at those graves I wonder if he remembered birthdays and parties and times when one of the kids came to him and said, "Daddy, who is God?" "Why do you talk to Him?" I wonder if Job remembered rocking them to sleep at night and holding them and getting up with them when they were sick? He lost it all. How does a person get through that kind of suffering? Chapter 2 doesn't answer that question; instead the first ten verses offer two more blows.

2. *Job lost his health.*

Look at 2:1-8.

> On another day the angels came to present themselves before the LORD, and Satan also came with them to present himself before him. And the LORD said to Satan, "Where have you come from?" [The question is for our benefit, not God's.]
> Satan answered the LORD, "From roaming through the earth and going back and forth in it." [A person without a relationship with God is restless.]
> Then the LORD said to Satan, "Have you considered my servant Job? There is no one on earth like him; he is blameless and upright, a man who fears God and shuns evil. And he still maintains his integrity, though you incited me against him to ruin him without any reason."
> "Skin for skin!" Satan replied. [Satan is saying, "The test isn't over. Let me do something to his body and he'll say good-by to you."] "A man will give all he has for his own life. But stretch out your hand and strike his flesh and bones, and he will surely curse you to your face."
> The LORD said to Satan, "Very well, then, he is in your hands; but you must spare his life."

37

So Satan went out from the presence of the Lord and afflicted Job with painful sores from the soles of his feet to the top of his head. Then Job took a piece of broken pottery and scraped himself with it as he sat among the ashes.

I circled the word "ruin" in my Bible and the word "incited." Strong words! It sounds like Satan has led God astray, but the Hebrew word translated "incited" seems to hold the thought that Satan instigated this evil against Job and God simply said, "Make your point. Job will not deny me." The word "ruin" literally means "to destroy," or "to swallow up." So Job not only lost his wealth, he also lost his health. The practical side of all of this is the sober fact that Job lost any means of earning a living and getting his life back together.

Let me help us get some idea of what Job endured by reading for you Dr. Meredith Kline's observation.

Modern medical opinion is not unanimous in its diagnosis of Job's disease, but according to the prognosis in Job's day, it was apparently hopeless. The horrible symptoms included inflamed eruptions accompanied by intense itching (2:7,8), maggots in ulcers (7:5), erosion of the bones (30:17), blackening and falling off of skin (30:30), and terrifying nightmares (7:14), though some of these may possibly be attributed to the prolonged exposure that followed the onset of the disease. Job's whole body, it seems, was rapidly smitten with the loathsome, painful symptoms.[2]

The picture here in 2:8 is horrifying. Keil and Delitzsch note, "The body is so affected, that some of the limbs fall off. Scraping with pottery will not only relieve the intolerable

---

[2]M.G. Kline, *Wycliffe Bible Commentary*, edited by Charles F. Pfeiffer and E.F. Harrison (Chicago: Moody Press, 1962), p. 463 has an excellent article on the subject of Job's physical condition.

itching . . . , but also remove the matter."[3] Some commentators believe Job was afflicted with smallpox, some are persuaded he had some terrible form of leprosy called "black leprosy," while many believe he had elephantiasis.

Whatever it was that Job encountered was something out of the Twilight Zone. He itched. He lost his appetite. He was depressed. He fought with flies and inevitable worms. He had extreme difficulty breathing. He lost weight. He was in constant pain and always feverish. It's all documented in his own words. Job is sitting outside the city he loved, where he was once a living legend, inhabiting the place where the garbage and manure were taken and burned.

How does a person get through stuff like that? How does someone like Corrie Ten Boom get through a concentration camp? How does a person get through broken health? Easy answers, if there are any, would be incredibly disrespectful and profoundly inaccurate. While we can hardly conceive an answer let me introduce you to the third blow that falls on Job.

3. Job lost his only support.

You wouldn't believe this unless you read it yourself. Job 2:9 is difficult to digest. "His wife said to him, 'Are you still holding on to your integrity? Curse God and die!'" How would you like to be married to someone like that? Ladies, how would you like it if you were in the hospital about to go in for surgery, the doctors say you have a ten percent chance of coming out alive and this husband of yours turns to you in your most vulnerable moment and says, "Where's the safety deposit key so I can get your life insurance policy out and by

---

[3]C.F. Keil and F. Delitzsch, *Commentary On The Old Testament*, Vol. 4, *Job* (Grand Rapids: Eerdmans, 1980 reprint). Translated by Francis Bolton.

the way, can my sister have your clothes if you don't make it?" You might recover long enough to shoot him!

Job's wife is only mentioned one other time in the entire story and that's in 19:17. Apparently Mrs. Job has come to visit again and her only comment is, "Your breath stinks." Job says, "My breath is offensive to my wife." Talk about trouble coming in threes. Some of the commentators are very hard on Job's wife. The early commentators and preachers were downright vicious. Chrysostom called her "the devil's best scourge." Augustine dubbed her "the devil's advocate." John Calvin got right to the heart of it. He said she was "the embodiment of Satan." There is something not fair about those statements. At best, what Mrs. Job tells her husband to do in 2:9 is a sincere desire to see his suffering stop. She doesn't see any possibilities of recovery. That is real life assessment. There isn't a person among us who hasn't said something really stupid to someone hurting. Job responds to his wife in 2:10. "You are talking like a foolish woman." He is not saying she is stupid. The word used by Job, "foolish," simply means that Mrs. Job lacked spiritual insight. She is deficient in understanding of spiritual matters. Can we prepare for encounters like Job's? Most of us know there aren't any easy answers. It probably is right to remember a few basic first-aid steps when we encounter a headline collision with suffering.

1. Prepare in advance. A person can't wait until all hell breaks loose before drawing on heavenly help. Get to know God deeply. Spend time in Scripture. Surround yourself with a few friends who are closer than a brother or sister. How I live right now will determine how I do when bad times come in threes.

2. Develop a good theology of God. Job seems to have known of God's loving lordship over all of life. God is full of grace. He can do no evil. He can take whatever suffering we are experiencing and make good of it. And if we discern that

we're suffering because of our own sin or poor judgment let's remind ourselves that God disciplines those He loves.

3. Recognize we are in a spiritual conflict. Modern science, technology, medicine are all good and helpful, but they can also dull our perspective. Some bad things are brought about by natural causes, but let us not forget that our enemy prowls around the world seeking whom he can devour (1 Pet. 5:8). He is our adversary (Eph. 6:10ff). Satan is real and he has been around a long time. Because he is a mortally wounded enemy, due to the cross of Christ, he is highly dangerous and angry. The promise of Scripture is that the One who lives in the Christian is greater than the one who lives in the world (1 John 4:4).

4. Don't withdraw. Don't retreat. If it is physically possible stay committed to being with other friends in Christ. I have watched people "die on the vine," not from what they were suffering, but from the lack of support and encouragement. Talk with somebody. Stay in circulation.

5. Look to the resurrection. That is exactly what Job did. In 19:25,26 Job declares, "I know that my Redeemer lives and that in the end He will stand upon the earth. And after my skin has been destroyed, yet, in my flesh I will see God; . . ." This is not some "pie in the sky" talk from Job. Eternal life begins right now. It started when I accepted Christ, by faith, as my Savior and Lord. The resurrection took care of the matter. Sometimes the thought that my life is securely in God's hands is the only thing that makes bad things seem manageable.

There is a profound question that looms over this section of Job. "Shall we accept good from God, and not trouble?" (2:10) I so appreciate Chuck Swindoll's response to this question. Here is some real wisdom.

Our great God isn't obligated to make us comfortable. . . . Are you ready to accept adversity? In the flesh, in the horizontal perspective, you'll resent it; you'll run from it;

41

you'll build up a bitterness against Him, saying, "What kind of a God is that?" But in the spiritual dimension, you will recognize that He has a right to bring the unpleasant as well as the pleasant. . . . Without this concept, you'll never be able to persevere through pressure. It will blow you away! Listen, our major goal in life is not to be happy or satisfied, but to glorify God.[4]

Job seems to somehow have known this great truth. The closing words of 2:10 simply read, "In all this, Job did not sin in what he said." I am crazy enough to believe, that in glorifying God, I am going to discover that my Redeemer, though seldom early, will never be late. He is in the business of "real life" even when pain comes packaged in threes, even if I have to wear my boots.

---

[4]Charles Swindoll, *Three Steps Forward Two Steps Back* (Nashville: Thomas Nelson, 1980), p. 57.

CHAPTER FOUR
God's First Aid
Job 2:11-13

"A friend is a trusted confidant to whom I am mutually drawn as a companion and an ally, whose love for me is not dependent on my performance, and whose influence draws me closer to God."[1]

Friends are never more important to us than when we are in trouble. When I was in the seventh grade my family moved to Peru, Indiana. I was the new kid on the block, attempting to cope with a Junior High School that was bigger than most of the towns where I had lived. I went out for football and made some friends. Ron Wilson. Bill Anderson. Mark Galbreath. John Garrett. Herbie Salaz. We ate hamburgers together. We played, lost and won together. It was in the course of that year that we were all in the same P.E. class.

The favorite form of exercise in the Boy's Physical Education program was a thing called "battle-ball." It was a game whose roots, I believe, went back to the gladiators in the coliseum of Rome. Maybe you have played the game. Sides are drawn up as evenly as possible. Each team gets half the gym. The balls that are to be used are all placed at center court. The whistle blows and a free-for-all ensues. Everybody with any courage seeks to get at least one ball and of course, avoid being hit with a blistering close-in assault. Both teams

---

[1]Jerry and Mary White, *Friends and Friendship* (Colorado Springs: NavPress, 1982), p. 13.

try to eliminate each other. If you are struck by a ball thrown from the opposing side you are out of the game. When only one person is left on each team the entire gym becomes the battlefield. There are no borders or boundaries.

One fateful day it came down to myself and one opposing player. The problem for me was that he was a bully and older than the rest of us. It is important to know that he was not the kind of bully who just threw out idle threats. He backed up his words with actions! He had fired several of the balls at me and narrowly missed taking off my head. In the heat of the moment I forgot who he was and I scooped up one of the balls he had thrown and I reared back and launched a "fiery dart." It was one of those throws that comes to a boy once in a lifetime. Straight, smooth and spinning toward the target like something launched by NASA the ball honed in on its objective. It seemed to defy gravity. It picked up speed. It appeared to have eyes and followed his every step. It whistled and hummed and exploded on the fat of his left thigh! The only thing redder than his leg was his face. Mr. Wernz, the P.E. teacher, blew the whistle for the end of class. I was pronounced the winner!

As we walked off the court the slain opponent uttered five simple words. By themselves those words are tame and gentle, but when packaged together they are chilling. The bully said, "I'll get you after school." One of my classmates offered these words of encouragement, "I'd go home now if I were you." I headed to the locker room to shower and the bully obviously wasn't finished with his threats. He said, "I'm going to kill you." "I'll be there," I said, which was really a dumb comeback. Who else would be there? He wanted to slay me, not the President. But it never happened. You know why? Because when the bully taunted me, my friends, Ronnie, Mark, Bill, John and Herbie surrounded him and declared, "We'll be there too!" Friends are not just gifts from God, but they can be first aid in seasons of trouble. The bully of the seventh grade class never bothered me again. It is always better to stick together.

In the story of Job there is a petite three verse section that can be easily overlooked in the overall narrative. It's all about friendship and times of trouble. Good friends, true friends know what to do when suffering strikes one of their own.

1. Develop a simple strategy.

Job 2:11 reads this way. "When Job's three friends, Eliphaz the Temanite, Bildad the Shuhite and Zophar the Naamathite, heard about all the troubles that had come upon him (Job), they set out from their homes and met together by agreement to go and sympathize with him and comfort him." We know very little, if anything, about Job's three buddies. Most of what we know is right here in the text. These three men lived in three different towns, maybe in three different countries. They got word that their friend was in trouble and they dropped what they were doing, packed their belongings, kissed the wife and children good-by, met in a pre-arranged location and developed their strategy. Do you have any friends like that?

Sometimes the Bible is as powerful in what it implies as it is in what it directly says. Though the Scriptures don't tell us directly these three friends of Job would never have come to his side if he had not meant something to them. Somewhere, somehow a friendship had grown that miles and times couldn't choke out. The Bible doesn't tell us how it all came about. Maybe they first met at a university in the East, perhaps in a class, Wisdom 101. We simply do not know how their lives were first cemented together. A friendship had been birthed. They were godly men who wanted to love God and know Him.

Job 2:11 tells us that this fraternity of men decided to go to Job's aid and do two things. First, they wanted to sympathize with him. The King James Version uses the word "mourn." Something gets lost in the translation from Hebrew to English. The word originally meant, "to move back and forth," like the moving and swaying of the head. The word came to mean, "to feel intense pity, to be sorry." The Hebrews combined these two ideas. They would show and feel when someone was hurting by moving their heads in a rocking motion. Leonard Copper, in *The Theological Word-book of the Old Testament*, says, ". . . It came to be a sign of pity . . . a sign of pity that sympathizes with one and recognizes the magnitude of the evil."[2] Job's friends decided to show their sympathy. Second, the verse tells us they also decided to comfort Job. The word used originally meant "to breathe deeply." It is a word that describes the physical display of feelings, like hugs, tears, holding hands, kissing or touching. These good men went to feel in some way what Job felt and to display somehow their love for him. That's a pretty good plan. Simple and gracious. So they went with their strategy in hand. Once they arrived at their friend's side they did a second thing which all true companions must do.

2. Openly Identify.

"When they saw him (Job's three friends saw him) from a distance, they could hardly recognize him; they began to weep aloud, and they tore their clothes, and sprinkled dust on their heads" (Job 2:12). These loyal friends didn't hide their feelings. They openly expressed their grief and sadness for Job through two Hebrew signs of mourning. They ripped their clothing and threw dust on their heads. I greatly appreciate the painful

---

[2]Leonard Copper, *The Theological Wordbook of The Old Testament*, Vol. 2, Edited by R.L. Harris, G.L. Archer and B.K. Waltke. (Chicago: Moody Press, 1980), p. 561. The word "nud" basically paints a picture of movement back and forth. The quote is actually taken from Kiel and Delitzsch's comments on Psalm 69:20.

clarity of David McKenna as he describes the scene of a sad reunion between Job and his friends.

> They are loyal friends who come with good intentions to comfort a brother in need. . . . His 3 visitors peer at Job but see nothing that resembles the Job they know. . . . They had not expected the sight of "walking death" that greets them. Job's friends come to the same conclusion as Job's wife — he might as well be dead. . . . As with a terminally ill patient for whom the doctor leaves the order, "Make him as comfortable as possible," Job's friends conclude that the compassion of mourning is the greatest comfort they can give.[3]

These three comrades openly identify with Job when others can't or won't. Do you recall Rudyard Kipling's, "The Thousandth Man?"

> One man in a thousand, Solomon says,
> will stick more close than a brother.
> And it's worthwhile seeking him half your days
> if you find him before the other.
> Nine hundred and ninety-nine depend
> on what the world sees in you,
> but the Thousandth Man will stand your friend
> with the whole round world against you . . .
> His wrong's your wrong, and his right's your right,
> in season or out of season . . .
> . . . but the Thousandth Man will stand by your side
> to the gallows-foot — and after![4]

---

[3]David L. McKenna, *The Communicator's Commentary*, Edited by Lloyd J. Ogilvie, Vol. XII (Waco: Word, 1986), pp. 47-48.

Dr. McKenna's theme is that of "seeing through suffering." He uses this in two primary ways. First, he interprets this to mean endurance and perseverance. Secondly, McKenna uses the phrase to mean keeping our eyes of faith on the One who walks with us through suffering.

[4]Rudyard Kipling, from *A Selection of His Stories and Poems*, edited by John Beecroft (New York: Doubleday, 1956).

Bildad, Eliphaz and Zophar were that thousandth man who openly identified with their friend in need. That is first aid in its finest form! There is a third application a person can carry out for someone in need when suffering strikes. This one is probably the most forgotten or misplaced.

3. Recognize our limitations.

Read Job 2:13. "Then they sat on the ground with him for seven days and seven nights. No one said a word to him, because they saw how great his suffering was." Extraordinary! Sometimes silence and presence are the two greatest gifts we can offer a hurting friend. Did you notice that word "suffering?" It is a word that emphasizes the mental anguish, the side of suffering that is intellectually painful. When these friends saw this kind of heartache they didn't speak a single word. They closed their mouths, opened their hearts and sat alongside their friend. Seven entire days went by! This was the time allotted for mourning the dead.

Some of you will recognize the name, Joe Bayly, former president of David C. Cook Publishing Company, editor, writer, preacher, and Church Statesman. If you know his story you know that during his life he lost three sons: an infant to cystic fibrosis, a five year old to leukemia, and a nineteen year old with hemophilia to a sledding accident. In spite of all the suffering he never wore the "martyr complex." He and his wife went on living as best they could. He wrote a book after the death of one of his sons called, *The View From A Hearse*. Read his advice.

> Don't try to "prove" anything to a survivor. An arm about the shoulder, a firm grip of the hand, a kiss: these are the proofs grief needs, not logical reasoning. I was sitting, torn by grief. Someone came and talked to me of God's dealings, of why it happened, of hope beyond the grave. He talked constantly, he said things I knew were true. I was unmoved, except to wish

he'd go away. He finally did. Another came and sat beside me. He didn't talk. He didn't ask leading questions. He just sat beside me for an hour or more, listened when I said something, answered briefly, prayed simply, left. I was moved. I was comforted. I hated to see him go.[5]

That's helpful counsel and profoundly insightful. C.S. Lewis said something akin to Bayly in his great book, *A Grief Observed*. After his wife, Joy, died from cancer Lewis wrote:

> There is a sort of invisible blanket between the world and me. I find it hard to take in what anyone says. Or perhaps, hard to want to take it in. It is so uninteresting. Yet I want the others to be about me. I dread the moments when the house is empty. If only they would talk to one another and not to me.[6]

Sometimes the very best first aid I can bring to a hurting friend is to recognize my own limitations and stand beside the sufferer. I have often asked myself, "What can I do for my friend?" I know I can pray simply and humbly. I know I can pay attention to practical things that need to be done or I can ask if there is anything I can do. I know, also, that I can cry with them and speak when spoken to. When Lois Clapp became so desperately ill that she could no longer attend Sunday worship she grieved over the loss. Not only did the cancer deprive her of work, but it also stole from her that which she loved deeply, to worship with her friends. Her friends decided that if Lois could not come to them they would go to her.

On a preselected Sunday, after morning worship, several hundred of us drove over to the Clapp home. We sang,

---

[5]Joe Bayly, *The View from a Hearse* (Elgin, IL: David C. Cook, 1973), pp. 40-41.

[6]C.S. Lewis, *A Grief Observed* (New York: Bantam Books, 1961), p. 1. What Lewis seems to be calling for is a friend's presence and availability.

prayed and stood silently as a witness of our love for their family. After we had sung several songs Bud, Lois and Troy came out of the house. Steve was away at college. Bud held Lois and we simply sang to God for people who couldn't. There have been a few moments in my life when I thought the Church was really being the Church. This was one of those occasions. There were more tears than there were handkerchiefs.

Neighbors came out to see what all the singing was about. Traffic stopped. It was a holy moment. As we started to leave I went up to Lois to simply give one more expression of love. I will never forget what she whispered in my ear through the mask that was present to protect her weakened body. She softly said, "You have no idea what this means to me." I knew I didn't. What could I say? I wish with all my heart that Job's three friends had continued their vigil of presence and silence, but the story doesn't end there.

The amazing thing is that God is the one who remains silent, who sits with Job and waits quietly, while the three friends break their silence and nearly ruin a lifelong friendship. After all is said and done, only God can perform the surgery that is needed. First aid isn't adequate. Only the Father in heaven can restore fractured joy. The good news is that He wants to do that very thing. He is seldom early to the surgical room of our hearts, but He is certainly never late, especially through friends who understand that silence can be golden.

CHAPTER FIVE
The Gift Nobody Wants
Job 3

"I have seen great beauty of spirit in some who were great sufferers. I have seen men, for the most part, grow better not worse with advancing years, and I have seen the last illness produce treasures of fortitude and meekness from most unpromising subjects. . . . Pain is a common and definite event. . . . Pain provides an opportunity for heroism; the opportunity is seized with surprising frequency."[1]

If you could have three wishes what would they be? Do you recall the story of Aladdin and his magic lamp? I love the part where the lamp is rubbed for the first time and the Genie bellows in a thunderous voice, "Say whatsoever thou wantest of me! Here am I, the slave to whoso holdeth the lamp." Aladdin responds in wonder, "O slave of the lamp, I am hungry and desire something to eat." The Genie would vanish in the twinkling of an eye and suddenly reappear "with a large silver tray bearing golden platters of various meats, delicate dainties, snow-white bread, and two silver cups with as many silver bottles containing sweet and dry wine."[2] A boy doesn't get a lunch like that very often!

Every single occasion that Aladdin made a wish the Genie

---

[1]C.S.Lewis, *The Problem of Pain*, pp. 108, 155 and 157.

[2]Richard F. Burton, *Aladdin and His Wonderful Lamp* (New York: Random House, 1993), p. 9.

would say, "To hear is to obey." People seldom talk like that or think like that anymore. Remember when we were kids how we use to ask each other, "If you had three wishes what would they be?" A hungry boy might say, "I would wish for french fries, a hamburger and coke under my pillow each night." He would drift off to sleep with his hand located in just the right place in case the dream came true. Someone might say, " I would wish for nice clothes, lots of money and to be liked." My friend, Jimmy Camper, might say, "I'd wish for a room full of candy, a Schwinn bike, and a zillion dollars!"

There is always someone who would wish for joy, peace and happiness, but few of us would take that request seriously. It is a funny thing about wishes, though — what I might wish for today isn't what I would wish for tomorrow. Everything changes when we come into a troubled time of suffering.

Sometimes I wish the Bible would give us more insight, more details into what happened between chapter 2 and chapter 3 of Job. Something occurred between Job's friends coming and sitting with him in silence (chapter 2) and his crying out in pain (chapter 3). I think David McKenna is correct. "Job realizes that they (his 3 friends) come not to help him, but to bury him. This is when all the doubt and despair that have been building up in Job explode in a torrent of anguish and anger."[3] In Job 3 the first words of this sufferer are recorded. He asks for three wishes. Here is the first wish and listen to what follows.

Wish #1. "I wish I were never born."

After this (7 days and 7 nights of mourning) Job opened his mouth and cursed the day of his birth. He said, "May the day

---

[3]McKenna, *The Communicator's Commentary*, p. 52.

of my birth perish and the night it was said, 'A boy is born!' That day, may it turn to darkness; may God above not care about it; may no light shine upon it. May darkness and deep shadow claim it once more; may a cloud settle over it; may darkness overwhelm its light. That night, may thick darkness seize it; may it not be included among the days of the year nor be entered in any of the months. May that night be barren; may no shout of joy be heard in it. May those who curse days curse that day, those who are ready to rouse Leviathan. May its morning stars become dark; may it wait for daylight in vain, and not see the first rays of dawn, for it did not shut the doors of the womb on me to hide trouble from my eyes."

This is a poem of grief. Job wishes that his mother had never conceived him. In 3:7 he uses the word "barren." It is a word that describes something stony or hard in an agricultural sense. When something was barren it meant no seed could grow. The soil didn't have the capacity to produce a crop. Job is wishing that his mother were sterile, that the sperm and egg had never joined and formed his life. He uses strange language in 3:9 to further explain his wish. There was a belief that sorcerers and magicians could make a day unlucky. There were many who were persuaded that these people could drum up Leviathan, a dragon, a sea monster. Some thought that this beast was seven-headed and could swallow the sun. Therefore, Job wishes that this creature could gobble up the day of his birth. The language is so vivid and colorful. In 3:9 Job literally declares that the day of his birth be a day that did "not see the eyelids of the morning." Thirteen times he uses the word "may." It functions as a curse uttered through clenched fists and gritted teeth. "I wish I were never born." That is Job's first wish as he pounds the ground.

A person can lose a mate and wish what Job did. A person can lose a job, face the humiliation of being fired and say what Job said. A person can drop a game winning touchdown pass and never get over it. A person can go through a relationship breaking up and identify with Job's request.

53

People can experience all kinds of pain and find that they agree with Job's first wish. It doesn't take much to identify with Job. Most of us are very fragile.

Wish #2. *"I wish I were dead."*

Job is saying, "If I can't stop the process of birth I wish that I could stop the process of my life right now." Here are Job's own words (3:11-19).

> Why did I not perish at birth, and die as I came from the womb? Why were there knees to receive me and breasts that I might be nursed? For now I would be lying down in peace; I would be asleep and at rest with kings and counselors of the earth, who built for themselves places now lying in ruins, with rulers who had gold, who filled their houses with silver.

Job is saying that death equalizes everything. He envies kings and wise men, even the wicked are to be envied (3:17), because nothing bad happens when you are buried. It is a democracy. All inequalities are evened up. Read on.

> Or why was I not hidden in the ground like a stillborn child, like an infant who never saw the light of day? There the wicked cease from turmoil and there the weary are at rest. Captives also enjoy their ease; they no longer hear the slave driver's shout. The small and the great are there, the slave is freed from his master.

If "may" is the key word in 3:3-10, then the key word in 3:11-19 is "why." Job is despairing. He asks the universal question, "Why me?" He simply wishes that he were dead. If we look at Job's words closely we can see a progression. "I wish I had died at birth (3:11), but since I did not, I wish I had died when I was being nursed by my mother (3:12), but since none of this happened I now wish I were dead" (3:13-19). Lots of people have said the same thing Job did. Elijah understood. "I have had enough, Lord. Take my life. I'm no better than my ancestors" (1 Kings 19:4).

The prophet spoke those words during a very difficult time in his ministry. The wicked Jezebel had threatened his life. Elijah needed food and rest. He had misplaced his divine perspective. Jonah understood Job's wish. "O Lord, take away my life, for it is better for me to die than to live" (Jonah 4:3). The preacher of Nineveh had come to the end of his rope. His hatred of the Ninevites (Assyrians) was so great that he couldn't stand it when they came to repentance! He had enough of God's grace! There isn't a single one of us who, at some point in life, hasn't wished or will wish what Job did.

Wish #3. "I wish it hadn't happened to me."

There it is in a nutshell. All that Job desires is found in this third wish (3:20-26).

> Why is light given to those in misery, and life to the bitter of soul, to those who long for death that does not come, who search for it more than for hidden treasure, who are filled with gladness and rejoice when they reach the grave? Why is life given to a man whose way is hidden, whom God has hedged in? For sighing comes to me instead of food; my groans pour out like water. What I feared has come upon me; what I dreaded has happened to me. I have no peace, no quietness; I have no rest, but only turmoil.

What Job is asking here is as real as it gets. He is saying in 3:1-10 that life is intolerable and in 3:11-19 that death is desirable, and now he wants an explanation. Why live anyway? In twentieth century jargon Job is saying, "I can't relax! I can't calm down! I can't sleep! I keep rehearsing it over and over in my mind. I wish this hadn't happened to me! I wish it hadn't happened to me!! I wish it hadn't happened to me!!!

I have a humble opinion that you can take or leave. I believe this last wish really got to the heart of God. I believe this because of what God will say later in the narrative. For now, if I could paint a picture of God's response I would have Him nodding His head, taking everything in, listening attentively, the way a mother can in the kitchen. A mom can hear the deep murmurings and songs of a teenager's soul, while peeling potatoes at the sink. I see God attending closely to every word Job utters, while carrying out His concern for the whole world. Perhaps He is taking care of some child's prayer who needs encouragement, but still listening to the man from Uz. If God wore glasses (not that I think He does), He would take them off, fold them up, tuck them away and look into the depths of Job's inner being with a probing stare that only a parent can have.

I am suggesting that Job just stepped into an area that he knows nothing about. Sometimes, in my spirit, I know that I just crossed over the line and God is going to set me straight. What Job is saying in his last wish is awfully close to saying, "If God were in charge of things, if He really cared, this would not have happened to me."

Perhaps the communists (I think their ideology is still around) have a keener understanding into suffering than most of us do. With scornful and arrogant attitudes they have cried, "Christianity is the opiate of the people." Their world-view leaves no room for God-centered thinking. They have looked upon the poor as the only people of value. Maybe they understand something that I forget. Poverty, as terrible as it is, is not altogether evil. Some good comes from it. Poverty can be evil and should be eradicated when possible, but it is also a gift that can bring clarity to a person's life. It doesn't often do that, but it can. Does that make sense? Suffering, as bad as it is, as much as I would wish it away, can bring me something good if I'll accept it. Hudson Taylor, great missionary to China in the 1800's, seems to have grabbed hold of this paradox. He came to a point in his life when he had to say good-by to his mother. Here is what he wrote. Listen to the suffering.

My beloved, now sainted, mother, had come to see me off from Liverpool. Never shall I forget that day, nor how she went with me into the little cabin that was to be my home for nearly six long months. With a mother's loving hand she smoothed the little bed. She sat by my side, and joined me in the last hymn that we should sing together before the long parting. We knelt down, and she prayed — the last mother's prayer I was to hear before starting for China. Then notice was given that we must separate, and we had to say good-by, never expecting to meet on earth again. For my sake she restrained her feelings as much as possible. We parted; and she went on shore, giving me her blessing; I stood along on deck, and she followed the ship as we moved toward the dock gates. As we passed through the gates, and the separation really began, I shall never forget the cry of anguish wrung from that mother's heart. It went through me like a knife. I never knew so fully, until then, what "God so loved the world" meant. And I am quite sure that my precious mother learned more of the love of God to the perishing in that hour than in all her life before.[4]

There is profound suffering in that farewell. But a few sentences later Hudson Taylor penned this single, glorious sentence.

Praise God, the number is increasing who are finding out the exceeding joys, the wondrous revelations of His mercies,

---

[4]Hudson Taylor, *Hudson Taylor*, Men of Faith series (Minneapolis: Bethany House, no date given). The book was previously published under the title, *To China With Love*. This is the autobiography of one of the most influential Christian missionaries of all times.

vouchsafed to those who "follow him," and emptying themselves, leave all in obedience to His great commission.[5]

In his heartache Taylor saw a gift. Can you see that? I am not saying that God brings pain into our lives and that is His gift to us. Pain and suffering come from a number of places. They can come from my own sin, from living in a fallen world, or from a direct attack of Satan or his forces, but God is not the source of pain and suffering. I am talking about a gift that comes to us when we get past the wish list and let God be God. I am speaking to myself as much as I am speaking to you. Jess Lair wrote a book worth reading simply because of its title, *Ain't I A Wonder And Ain't You A Wonder Too?*. Jess is quoting his friend Vince. Vince tells Jess,

> "If I want to live the abundant life, I've got to stop fighting for complete control. If you want to live abundantly, you must surrender. There ain't no money nor job nor power that can help you get rid of grief. You've got to accept God or be God" [And Jess remarks:] That's the simplest I've ever heard the matter put. You've got to accept some high power, some power outside yourself or you've got to be it. When you try being God, you're all the power there is.[6]

While working on this book I took a trip to the Philippines with a great group of ministers from throughout the United States. We were going to be a part of the first "Christ In Youth Conference" ever held in that region of the world. God blessed the trip greatly. When I returned I became very sick. I was stuck, poked, probed, medicated and examined by three different doctors. One of the physicians was an infectious disease specialist. I was tested for every kind of fever and disease known to be contracted in the Orient, from

---

[5]Ibid., p. 53.

[6]Jess Lair, *Ain't I A Wonder And Ain't You A Wonder Too?* (New York: Doubleday), 1977, pp. 53-54.

malaria to typhoid. I was cold one moment and hot the next. I had a rash all over my body that itched so badly I couldn't sleep. Once the medication took hold I was exhausted. Two weeks went by before I could begin to get out of bed. I really thought that death would be better than this! I can't possibly understand all that Job endured, but I think all of us have had enough of the taste of real life that we have a partial grasp of Job's plight.

About nine years ago I snuck away from the hectic pace of local church ministry in order to find a place where I could get some concentrated time for praying and planning. I ended up in the small town where I spent the large portion of my grade school years. The sky was blue, the clouds white and the sun warm. I parked my car alongside the school playground where I spent many happy days as a kid. I rolled down the windows of the car and began to work in my make-shift office. The school bell rang and children came out from everywhere for recess. Pieces of conversation began to fill the air. "Kick 'em in the shins. He's weird!" "I think I love him. Do you think he loves me?"

"Roger, your hair stinks today." I laughed and recalled the conversations I had participated in long ago. I drove over to Sullivan Street to see the old parsonage where I grew up. I parked the car in the alley that circles the block and I got out and walked down the railroad tracks toward the creek and woods where I used to play. Some strolls are almost sacred. I remembered how I had imagined myself to be Tom Sawyer on the Mississippi or Robin Hood in Sherwood Forest.

Of course, everybody knows everybody in a small town. I saw two people watching me. I didn't recognize them. They seemed to be talking about me. I didn't care and went on with my walk. I shuffled past the grain bins where the hum of fans could be heard drying out the corn and I could smell that sweet odor of grain. The noon siren sounded. I had not heard that whistle in years. That used to be my alarm clock, my cue, that it was lunch time. Time for tuna casserole and cold milk. The further I walked the further I strolled down memory lane. I saw signs of the old treehouse that I had attempted to build when I was eight years old. I went by the drug store. It's now a warehouse. Mark Donovan and I used to celebrate our friendship every Saturday morning with a nickel coke and a penny pretzel in that drug store. I recalled it all.

Right about then a pain hit me squarely in the middle of my heart. I remembered how I cried and pleaded with my parents to let me stay when they announced that we were moving away. The departure from that town became a gift from God that I never wanted. My love for people, my convictions about Jesus and life, my belief about God and purpose, all that I am grew out of that difficult childhood experience of farewell. When I stopped wishing to stay and moved away with my family I got a gift that no one really wants. One of the hardest and most difficult things to hear and believe is that God is present to hear all of our wishes. He knows what is best. He waits until we're ready to open the gift He truly wants to give us. Job isn't able to open the gift God offers yet. Sometimes I'm not ready either. The great gift-giver is seldom early, but never, never late.

CHAPTER SIX

Talks at the Dump: Round One Job 4-14

"What comes into our minds when we think about God is the most important thing about us. . . . The gravest question before the Church is always God Himself, and the most portentous fact about any man is not what he at a given time may say or do, but what he in his deep heart conceives God to be like."[1]

How do you sink a friendship? It was October and autumn still hadn't been muscled out by winter. The leaves were displaying all their colors and clapping their hands to the glory of God. There were two boys, good friends, who had spent the day bike riding and playing football at Bob White's house. They had eaten bologna sandwiches at half-time and drunk grape Kool-aid. It was the kind of day a person files away to use later on when life seems drab and boring. On their way home they began to plan the rest of the day. One of the boys said, "Let's go over to my house and throw the football some more. You need the practice." Without thought the other boy reacted, "You're the one who dropped more passes than a blind man with one hand!" An

---

[1]A.W. Tozer, *The Knowledge of The Holy* (San Francisco: Harper and Row, 1961), p. 1. Tozer is probably the most widely read devotional writer of the twentieth century. I highly recommend wide reading of this great Church Statesman who wrote this particular selection just two years prior to his death.

intellectual exchange followed that went something like this. "Did not!" "Did too!" "Didn't!" "Did!" One of the boys untied his jacket that was wrapped around his waist and lightly swung it at his friend. It was just a joke, but the zipper hit the tip of the friend's ear. An unplanned response came. "That was really stupid. Why are you so dumb sometimes?" The verbal stab seemed like an invitation for the boy with the jacket to repeat his imitation of Indiana Jones. He whipped his coat toward his friend. This time it had more velocity. They began to exchange words and punches. Pretty soon they couldn't remember how the fight had started and didn't much care. What mattered now was winning. What had started out as a pleasant fall day ended up as the first day of a broken friendship. They were never really friends again. Oh, they were cordial enough in the hallway at school, but never buddies. I know all about this divorce between two companions because I was one of the boys.

Job was a blessed man. He had three friends: Eliphaz, Bildad and Zophar. For some reason that isn't all that clear in the story these three friends felt compelled to respond to Job's words of pain. Each of them offers a piece of advice on why they believe their friend is suffering and how he should handle it. In turn Job reacts to each one of the three and sometimes, in pain and frustration, talks directly to God. The story moves rapidly from this point. The central concern of Job's friends are, "Why is Job suffering?" Three successive rounds of conversation follow. The sufferer from Uz is sitting out at the edge of town scraping himself with a piece of pottery. He has positioned himself around the garbage and manure piles that have been discarded. Let me introduce you to Job's three friends. The first is Eliphaz (4:1-8).

#1. Eliphaz: The voice of experience.

Then Eliphaz the Temanite replied: "If someone ventures a word with you, will you be impatient? But who can keep from speaking? Think how you have instructed many, how you have strengthened feeble hands. Your words have supported those who stumbled [Literally — "your words have kept people on their feet"]. You have strengthened faltering knees. But now trouble comes to you, and you are discouraged; it strikes you, and you are dismayed. Should not your piety be your confidence and your blameless ways your hope? Consider now: Who, being innocent, has ever perished? Where were the upright ever destroyed? As I have observed, those who plow evil and those who sow trouble reap it."

Eliphaz is saying, "If you are as righteous as you say you are, if your suffering hasn't been brought on by any sin, then why are you complaining?" This first friend sticks a subtle dagger into the heart of Job. He adds the clincher in 4:12. "A word was secretly brought to me, my ears caught a whisper of it." Eliphaz declares that he has received a vision which told him everything regarding Job's plight. His vision is found in chapter five of the narrative and can be summarized in three sentences.

1. Good people don't suffer.
2. Sin has brought this suffering into Job's life.
3. Repent and God will prosper Job's life again.

The central thesis or argument from Eliphaz is this: "Job, I've been where you are. I'm experienced. I have watched this kind of denial happen again and again." I want to be fair with this well meaning friend. Eliphaz seems to want to be gentle. He's probably the oldest in the group. He is rational and polite. He firmly believes he is speaking the truth, but his timing and his spirit are all wrong. In his own loving way Eliphaz tries to shame Job into submission. How do you question someone who says, "God has spoken to me"? Job doesn't even deal with it. His response to Eliphaz (Job 6,7) can be drawn together in two brief statements.

1. *Where are my friends when I need them?* Check out 6:13. "Do I have any power to help myself, now that success has

been driven from me? A despairing man should have the devotion of his friends, . . . But my brothers are as undependable as intermittent streams. . . ." Job closes his response to Eliphaz with a thud. To paraphrase Job 6:22-23, "Have I ever asked for help before?"

2. *Where have I been wrong?* Job is wondering what exactly he has done to deserve this kind of suffering. He asks, "Teach me and I will be quiet; show me where I have been wrong" (Job 6:24). So Eliphaz isn't much help to Job. Sometimes friends with experience end up hurting more than helping. Sometimes their well meaning words only sink a friendship further.

Job's second friend is Bildad. Let's call him:

#2. Bildad: the voice of tradition.

We don't have to read a great deal about this man. He sings from the same hymnal as Eliphaz. He simply sings with greater fervor and intensity. Bildad's speech to Job is found in Job 8. This second friend uses three illustrations to answer the question as to why Job is suffering. Bildad illustrates with papyrus (8:11), a spider's web (8:14-15), and a plant on rocky soil (8:16-19). He has one point and one point only. "Job, you are a hypocrite. You have sinned. Admit it." Papyrus needs a marsh to grow, a spider needs a web, and a plant on rocky soil needs to spread its roots in order to find water. The key idea is simple. Suffering needs sin. Sin causes suffering. Righteousness brings about prosperity.

In 8:2 Bildad reveals his bedside manner. "How long will you say such things ("How long will you declare your innocence")? Your words are a blustering wind." The Hebrew word for wind is the word translated "air in motion" or "an empty breath." To put it into contemporary language Bildad is suggesting to Job that he is "an old windbag!" If that didn't hurt enough Bildad brings back Job's most painful memory of all. Job 8:4 reads, "When your children sinned against him (God), he gave them over to the penalty of their sin." "Job, your kids died because they sinned against God." If Job could have stood up at that moment he might have punched Bildad into the next county. Bildad draws his argument primarily from tradition. Bildad says, "Ask the former generations and find out what their fathers learned . . ." (8:8). How do you question someone who says, "Ask your dead relatives . . . they'll set you straight"?

I would strongly encourage you to read Job's response to Bildad in chapters nine and ten. At times Job reaches heights of great eloquence as he describes God's power, especially in 9:5-10. Summaries are often dangerous and inaccurate, but if I were pressed to simplify Job's retort of Bildad's faulty reasoning it would look like this.

1. I am not wicked.
2. I am not being singled out by God. Even the righteous suffer.
3. I am deeply hurt.
4. I want to die.

The longing of this sufferer is seen in 9:33. "If only there were someone to arbitrate between us, to lay his hand upon us both." Because God is so great Job looks for someone to present his case before the Almighty. Bildad's help is nonexistent. There is a third friend who might be of some assistance. His name is Zophar.

However, this man violates everything that is proper and holy in a friendship. Here is the label I would attach to Zophar.

#3. Zophar: the voice of assumption.

Do you remember Dale Carnegie? He wrote a lot of insightful things on how to get along with people. He authored a little piece entitled, *12 Ways To Win People to Your Way of Thinking*. Rule #2 went something like this: "Show respect for the other person's viewpoint. Never tell someone he is wrong." I'm not sure I agree with all of that, but I am certain Zophar never heard of Carnegie and would not have read his book anyway. This third friend of Job tries to model his opinion after Eliphaz and Bildad, but he can't quite sing the same song. He simply yells at Job. Chapter eleven of the story is filled with shouting! Zophar, without reason of experience or tradition, assumes Job is guilty of something. He brutally tells Job, "Know this: God has even forgotten some of your sin" (Job 11:6). Translation: "Job, your punishment is even less than you deserve."

Ouch! The problem with statements like that and most of the declarations made by the other two friends is that they all carry with them some partial truth. When God gets framed up in some half-baked theology there is the danger of abuse and manipulation. Have you ever experienced that? Now and then, people come into our lives who use submission and authority as a means to change our thinking.

I deeply appreciate the writings of Gene Edwards. I sometimes find myself arguing with him, but I have learned so much from reading his books. One particular book, small but mighty, has reminded me of the way in which people try to manipulate through half-baked truths. Listen.

Take a man who does not hesitate to scare people out of their wits with two of the most powerful tools known to humanity. If you don't know what those two tools are, one of them is Scripture and the other one is God. When you threaten people with a Scriptural view of something and then tell them it will please (or displease) God, . . . Add to that the ingredient of total conformity by everyone to one set of morals, one set of social standards, and one set of clothing and you have a situation that is not only potentially harmful to brothers and sisters, you have a situation that probably cannot be justified from even the most extreme view of Scripture.[2]

Zophar's manipulative counsel is very simple. You can read it in full in Job 11:13-19. Here is the gist of it. "If you put away your sin, your suffering will end and health, wealth and prosperity will return." If that reminds you of any church, or group, or book you have read, take note and be warned. Some lies have very deep roots.

If the good friendship between Job and his three companions wasn't sunk before Zophar showed up it certainly was after he left. How do you talk with a friend who assumes you are guilty? Job gets so cranked up that he explodes.

> What you know, I also know; I am not inferior to you. But I desire to speak to the Almighty and to argue my case with God. You, however, smear me with lies; you are worthless physicians, all of you! If only you would be altogether silent! For you, that would be wisdom. Hear now my argument; listen to the plea of my lips. . . . Keep silent and let me speak (Job 13:2-5, 13).

Though I hate the words I do understand why Job says what he does. His angry speech could be reduced to six words: "Shut up and leave me alone." What follows in chapters thirteen and fourteen is Job talking to himself and with God. He has had enough of round one at the dump.

Friendship. All three of these men just wanted to help. Eliphaz, as gently as he could, said, "Job, I've been there and you're wrong." Bildad followed with, "It has always been this way. You are wrong." Zophar concluded the trilogy, "My common sense tells me you are wrong." Each of them urged

---

[2]Gene Edwards, *Letters to a Devastated Christian* (Goleta, CA: Christian Books, 1983 reprint), p. 18. I particularly have enjoyed and found helpful Edwards' book, *A Tale of Three Kings* (Augusta, ME: Christian Books, 1982 reprint).

Job to repent (5:8; 8:6; 11:14). According to the tribunal of wise men Job was guilty until proven innocent. This reminds me of something I once read in Mark Twain's classic, *The Adventures of Tom Sawyer*. Tom had been stealing sugar cubes from the sugar bowl. Aunt Polly had whacked him on each occasion. Tom complains:

"Aunt, you don't whack Sid when he takes it." "Well, Sid don't torment a body the way you do. You'd be always into that sugar if I warn't watching you." Presently she stepped into the kitchen, and Sid, happy in his immunity, reached for the sugar bowl — a sort of glorying over Tom which was well- nigh unbearable. But Sid's fingers slipped and the bowl dropped and broke. Tom was in ecstasies. In such ecstasies that he even controlled his tongue and was silent. He said to himself that he would not speak a word, even when his aunt came in, but would sit perfectly still till she asked who did the mischief; and then he would tell, and there would be nothing so good in the world as to see that pet model "catch it." He was so brimful of exultation that he could hardly hold himself when the old lady came back and stood above the wreck discharging lightnings of wrath from over her spectacles. He said to himself. "Now it's coming!" And the next instant he was sprawling on the floor! The potent palm was uplifted to strike again when Tom cried out: "Hold on, now, what 'er you belting me for? Sid broke it!" Aunt Polly paused, perplexed, and Tom looked for healing pity. But when she got her tongue again, she only said: "Umf! Well, you didn't get a lick amiss, I reckon. You been into some other audacious mischief when I wasn't around, like enough."[3]

How many friendships have been torpedoed and eventu-

---

[3]Mark Twain, *The Adventures of Tom Sawyer* (New York: Holt, Rinehart and Winston, in the *Great Books For Children* series, 1961 reprint), pp. 22-23. Mark Twain's writings, especially of Tom Sawyer and Huckleberry Finn were my favorite readings as a child. As I look back on it there is so much theology packed into those books.

ally sunk because someone assumed something that was not true? At the end of round one Job is still alone and still lonely. Job does three elementary things.

1. He clings to his own worth (13:2).
2. He pities his friends (13:4ff).
3. He turns to God again (13:20ff).

I would be terribly amiss if I didn't suggest some very practical applications on choosing godly friends and being a godly friend. With no comment I offer the following.

1. Be a friend and choose a friend who knows a God of grace. Watch out for legalists. They will reap a whirlwind in your life.
2. Be a friend and choose a friend who has deep biblical convictions, but doesn't flaunt them in a "holier than thou" fashion.
3. Be a friend and choose a friend who will speak the truth in love. No one can move through life maturely without this kind of friend.
4. Be a friend and choose a friend who continues to grow as a disciple of Jesus.

These eleven chapters (4-14) represent conversation at the edge of a town, in a community dump, between Job and his three buddies. It is more than just a treatise on friendship. It is about the kind of God we know. It is about how the kind of God we know affects our friendships, especially when trouble comes for a visit.

I would like to say something as firmly as I know how. For me that means that I am talking to you gently and in a whisper. Here it is. Unless I know this loving God who permits suffering, when pain comes my way and my friends screw up, unless I know that kind of God, I will sink the friendship with bitterness. Friends can be cruel. A sound biblical view of God is the fertile soil that grows relationships which resemble Eden prior to the Fall.

Everybody knows good ol' Charlie Brown. I love Charles Schultz's work. I particularly recall the day that Charlie Brown goes to see Dr. Lucy. He needs some psychiatric help. He needs some care, some love, a friend. Lucy tells Charlie Brown, "Cheer up, Charlie Brown; you have lots of friends. Look on the bright side of life. Don't be a blockhead. You've got friends." Charlie Brown's eyes look as if Lucy has given him the best present any human being could give another human being. In surprise Charlie says, "I do? You mean it? I have friends?" "Of course you do, Charlie Brown," Lucy responds. "I do, I do, I do," he says to himself, "I have lots of friends." And as he walks away with his head in the clouds Lucy taunts and ridicules him, "Name one, Charlie Brown, name one."

When C.S. Lewis found himself grieving over the death of his wife and dear friend he wrote these words:

> Not that I am (I think) in much danger of ceasing to believe in God. The real danger is coming to believe such dreadful things about Him. The conclusion I dread is not, "So there's no God after all," but "So this is what God's really like."[4]

The key to a friendship is so obvious. It is Christ at the center of that relationship. That's what Job wanted. Consider 9:33 again. "If only there were someone to arbitrate between us . . . ." The word for a person who arbitrates is the word for a judge or an umpire. Job wanted someone who could bring about a reasonable settlement to his awful circumstance. Jesus is that one (1 Tim. 2:5). It is no great secret, except to a lost world. Whether we believe in God or not, there is ample evidence to support the idea that he believes in us. Round one of talks at the dump resolves little. I do believe that God is watching and waiting in silence. He alone knows what being a true friend is all about. I long for what was said of

---

[4]C.S. Lewis, *A Grief Observed*, pp. 9-10.

Abraham to be said of me: "he was called God's friend" (2 Chron. 20:7 and James 2:23). To be God's friend means I obey Him and I go on obeying Him. Though God is seldom early, He is never late for me, even when I can hardly believe it.

CHAPTER SEVEN
Talks At The Dump:
Round Two
Job 15-21

"Write your criticisms in dust, your compliments in marble."[1]

How are we supposed to handle criticism when we are journeying through a season of suffering? Job has been assaulted with words. Job's three friends have sliced and cut into the heart of the one they came to console. Before he even has a chance to lick his wounds round two of talks at the dump begin. How does a godly person respond to a second wave of verbal attack? We don't know all that Job was feeling at this point in the story. Perhaps Joe Bayly's words fit this sufferer's plight.

I'm alone Lord — alone — a thousand miles from home. There's no one here who knows my name — except the clerk — and he spelled it wrong. No one to eat dinner with, laugh at my jokes, listen to my gripes, be happy with me about what happened today and say, "That's great." No one cares. There's just this lousy bed and slush in the street outside between the buildings. I feel sorry for myself and I've plenty of reason to. Maybe I ought to say, "I'm on top of it," "Praise the Lord," "Things are great," but they're not. Tonight it's all gray slush.[2]

---

[1]Charles Swindoll, *The Grace Awakening* (Dallas: Word, 1990), p. 175.

[2]Joe Bayly, *Psalms of My Life* (Wheaton: Tyndale House, 1969), p. 16.

Everyone has gray slush days. Job had a number of those days back to back. What made them so gray and slushy wasn't that he had lost his health, his farm, his ten children, his wealth, his position in the community. All of that was true and painful, but what really hurt was the criticism heaped upon him by those he loved. Do you recall what that kind of criticism feels like?

Miss Clutter was my fifth grade math teacher at the East Ward Grade School in Waynesburg, Pennsylvania. I do not wish to speak ill of the dead, but simply to recall a moment in my life when I tasted criticism and never forgot its bitter flavor. Miss Clutter seemed to me to be a very unhappy person. Perhaps she wasn't. I can't remember, though, a single time I ever heard her laugh. The only time I saw her smile was when Mr. Thompson, the principal, came by for a visit or when everyone sat quietly with both feet squarely planted on the floor. Order and structure pleased her. She smiled at good posture, discipline and correct answers. I thought her favorite line in Scripture might be, "there is no joy in Gilead."

I guess we never got off on the right foot. When my family moved from Heyworth, Illinois to Waynesburg there were a lot of adjustments. New house, dad's new work, new town, new faces, new culture, new school and new friends. I loved school, until I met Miss Clutter and overnight I lost my love. I think it started the day she began correcting my speech. She was not an admirer of my flat, midwestern accent. I'd say, "su-prise" and she would correct me with "*sur-prise.*" I would say, " I have a wusshh." Miss Clutter would respond, "No you don't! You have a *wish.*"

I often wondered if she had been one of those poor souls who had been left standing at the wedding altar. Maybe she wanted to be a brain surgeon and somewhere along the educational highway she ran out of gas. Maybe she failed a course and wound up teaching fifth grade math and hated it.

I don't know what made her appear so unhappy.

The day that stands out in my mind was the day she criticized me in front of the class. We had been working on fractions and common denominators. From time to time she would call a student to the chalkboard and have that student walk through the problem explaining the steps and how they arrived at the answer. She called Ronnie Hart up to the board and he did fine. He was a good student and a good friend. However, he didn't get along with Miss Clutter very well. He would create songs and poetry about her that I wouldn't repeat today. They were silly, even stupid, but I thought they were funny.

I must have been thinking about one of those songs when I heard my name called. I had no idea what Miss Clutter wanted and she knew it. I got to the front of the class, picked up the chalk and stared into space. "You have no idea what you're supposed to be doing, do you?" Miss Clutter asked. She had me cold. "Daydreaming, weren't you?" "Yes," I squeaked. "Is that a subject they teach in Illinois?" She demanded to know. "Maybe," I defiantly said.

That was the wrong answer! Miss Clutter pulled out her pointy little index finger in front of my big fifth grade nose and almost in a shout she declared, "You get smart with me and I'll call your parents and we'll have a visit with Mr. Thompson. You're in Pennsylvania now and we work here and you had better catch up. We're not a bunch of country bumpkins. This class can't afford to wait on you."

If I had not been so afraid of my father's discipline I think I would have walked out of the class that day and never come back. I never worked at math again. I got by. But I never learned what I could have. There is nothing as lethal as negative criticism. Even as I write I pause in prayer and reflection that I could still carry around inside of me an episode that took place thirty plus years ago.

We are in round two of conversation at the town dump. Job continues to ponder his innocence and his three friends persist in trying to answer the formidable question: Why is Job suffering?

Allow me to further introduce you to Eliphaz, Bildad and Zophar. I particularly want to point out their criticisms and the manner in which Job responds. A word of reminder: round two is not just a brief on how to handle criticism even though it sounds very much like that.

The first person to speak is Eliphaz. Remember that he is the voice of experience. All three of Job's friends will enlarge their theology of suffering. Eliphaz defines his perspective in four words.

#1. Only the wicked suffer.

His words to Job are found in the fifteenth chapter. This time his vocabulary is more severe, less gentle, less diplomatic. Eliphaz's sharp criticism cuts Job to the quick. "Job, because my experience shows that only the wicked suffer, you must be wicked." Listen to Job 15:4.

> But you even undermine piety and hinder devotion to God. Your sin prompts your mouth; you adopt the tongue of the crafty. Your own mouth condemns you, not mine; your own lips testify against you.

Eliphaz criticizes Job for godless talk. He rebukes Job, "If you were as innocent as you claim, you would keep your mouth shut." Then to add insult to injury Eliphaz asks (Job 15:12-16),

> Why has your heart carried you away, and why do your eyes flash, so that you vent your rage against God and pour out such words from your mouth? What is man, that he could be pure, or one born of woman, that he could be righteous? If

God places no trust in his holy ones, if even the heavens are not pure in his eyes, how much less man, who is vile and corrupt, who drinks up evil like water!

Job's friend uses two of the strongest words he could dig up to describe the nature of people. In 15:16 Eliphaz speaks of the "vile" nature of man. The KJV translates the word "abominable." The Hebrew word used here could be translated detestable, hateful, horrible, revolting or even shameful, depending upon the context. The second word used by Eliphaz is the word "corrupt." It means filthy, morally corrupt, impure, but originally it was a word used to describe what happened to milk after it sat out too long. It would turn sour. Eliphaz is about as gracious and sensitive as Major Frank Burns of *M.A.S.H.* fame. Even though he is speaking of people in general as having "gone sour," Eliphaz is telling Job, "If the shoe fits, wear it! It must be your size, because only the wicked suffer!" Everything else that this friend says is an offshoot of previous statements and everything else spoken by Zophar and Bildad will be built upon what Eliphaz concludes with in this section. In summary Eliphaz adds three cutting criticisms of Job.

1. You are not wise (15:1-13).
2. You are not innocent (15:14-16).
3. You are not correct (15:17,18).

I'll come back to how Job handled this criticism in a moment. For now lets add Bildad's criticism and belief to our list.

#2. *"The wicked **always** suffer."*

Job 18:1-21 is Bildad's second round of talk. He adds nothing new to his previous statements. He once again tries to frighten Job into repentance and from 18:5 on he uses twisted quotations and proverbs to prove his point. In 18:14-19 Bildad brings into play the cruelest means of confronting

Job. He does what we all do sometimes in the heat of the moment. Bildad digs up the past. If I really want to criticize someone I don't have to dream up something; I can simply dredge up their past. Because all of us have enough dumb things in our lives that could be easily used against us, it is not difficult to frame up some very juicy criticisms. Bildad ties an ugly knot of half-truths and myth. Job is directly linked to the wicked.

18:14 "He (the wicked) is torn from the security of his tent." Translated: "Job, you lost your house, didn't you?"

18:15 "Fire resides in his tent." Translation: "Job, fire came down and burned up your sheep and servants, didn't it?"

18:17 "The memory of him perishes from the earth." Translation: "Job, people don't even recognize you any more. I didn't recognize you when I saw you. How long have we known each other?"

18:19 "He has no offspring or descendants among his people, no survivor where once he lived." Translation: "Job, what happened to your ten children? Have you seen them lately?"

Wow! Talk about an unfair fight! Bildad's final word of encouragement summarizes his whole viewpoint. Once again in speaking of the wicked Bildad describes Job as the tragic example of how the wicked *always* suffer (18:20,21).

> Men of the west are appalled at his fate; men of the east are seized with horror. Surely such is the dwelling of an evil man; such is the place of one who knows not God.

Bildad's conclusion is a knife in the back of Job. "Job, you are wicked and you do not know God." In Bildad's mind the question is settled and completely answered. The debate is over. Why do the wicked suffer according to this second friend? They suffer because they get paid in full for their wicked deeds. Again, before we hear Job's response let's listen to Zophar's second speech. His criticism is closely related to Bildad's.

#3. *"The wicked's prosperity is short-lived."*

Job 20 records Zophar's words of advice to his friend. If we tore apart Zophar's speech and analyzed it as if it were a sermon it would be stylistically and sermonically a masterpiece. Zophar has three points he wants to present.

1. The joy of the wicked is brief (20:6-11).
2. The sin of the wicked is self-destructive (20:12-19).
3. The judgment of God is sure (20:20-28).

End of sermon. As far as Zophar is concerned all is well. Job is guilty. He implies that Job got all his wealth by ripping off people. He took what wasn't his. But Zophar offers no proof, no evidence, no hope, no motive. And at times he is just plain crude.

> Though his pride reaches to the heavens and his head touches the clouds, he will perish forever, like his own dung; those who have seen him will say, "Where is he?" (20:6,7)

How does a person handle that kind of criticism? Job's example might just save us the next time we're suffering from a previous wound and along comes a friend with a round of criticism. It is time to listen to Job's response. This is what he does and what I must do.

#1. *Admit the hurt.*

Don't bury the pain. Don't deny it. Acknowledge what is hurting us. Job models that again and again. When Eliphaz blasted Job in chapter 15 Job responds in chapters 16 and 17 with some of his most transparent statements.

79

16:6 "Yet if I speak, my pain is not relieved; and if I refrain, it does not go away."

17:1 "My spirit is broken (Talk about transparency. A person doesn't get any more open and honest than that), my days cut short, the grave awaits me."

17:7 "My eyes have grown dim with grief."

17:11 "My days have passed, my plans are shattered, and so are the desires of my heart."

InterVarsity publishes a little booklet entitled, *Practical Criticism: Giving It and Taking It,* by John Alexander. Maybe you have read it. He offers eleven rules on how to receive negative criticism. Rule #11 is "Talk About It." Listen to this practical gem.

> The talking cure is especially helpful — talking first to God in prayer, talking then with other persons who will listen. If they understand enough to offer suggestions, so much the better. But even if they offer nothing in response, the very fact that they listen contributes immeasurably in helping the criticized person carry the burden.[3]

Job, in spite of all his suffering, is able to articulate and admit his hurt. He talks about it. I don't know if you read the writings of Henri Nouwen. He is a Catholic priest, psychologist, teacher, caretaker, and a humble man of God. He has taught at Notre Dame and Yale Divinity School. He is a crisp and insightful writer who combines precise thinking with an extremely caring spirit. In reflecting on a past experience in his own life he wrote these helpful words.

> I hardly remember what it was, but a small critical remark and a few irritations during my work in the bakery were enough to tumble me head over heels into a deep, morose mood. Many

---

[3]John Alexander, *Practical Criticism: Giving It and Taking It* (Downers Grove: IVP, 1976), p. 29.

hostile feelings were triggered and in a long sequence of morbid associations, I felt worse and worse about myself, my past, my work, and all the people who came to mind. But happily I saw myself tumbling and was amazed how little was needed to lose my peace of mind and to pull my whole world out of perspective. Oh, how vulnerable I am![4]

Job portrays raw honesty as he walks through his season of suffering. There is a second way in which he models dealing genuinely with criticism.

#2. Stand honorably.

When the critics came to "help" him deal with his suffering Job dug in. He stood firm. He held fast. When Eliphaz said, "Only the wicked suffer," Job countered with, "The righteous suffer too" (Job 16 & 17). When Bildad said, "The wicked always suffer," Job declared, "Many wicked people escape suffering in this life" (Job 19). When Zophar said, "The wicked's prosperity is short-lived," Job spoke up, "Sometimes the wicked's prosperity gets passed on to their children" (Job 21). He stood honorably on each occasion. I especially love Job's response in 19:4, "If it is true that I have gone astray, my error remains my concern alone."

There is a third way we can handle untimely criticism by looking at Job's example.

#3. Keep your sense of humor.

It is easy to miss some of Job's humor in all the tragedy, but it is present in the narrative.

---

[4]Henri Nouwen, *The Genesee Diary* (Garden City, NY: Image Books, 1976), p. 57. Nouwen is one of those rare writers who allows you to see into and explore his soul. He gives me such hope.

81

Listen to Job's reflection on God as he pours out his frustration.

> His anger burns against me; he counts me among his enemies. His troops advance in force; they build a siege ramp against me and encamp around my tent (Job 19:11,12).

Job paints this picture of God working against him. He feels that God has brought this huge army, this monstrous force, a battalion of Rambos, and totally surrounded one man. God has seemingly set all His great weaponry against one tent. The Lord Almighty, according to Job, has built a road up to his pup tent, with all His battering machines, in order to break it down. In cartoon fashion Job shows us the fortress of one tent against a regiment of Green Berets! It is very much like taking a shotgun in hand in order to kill flies on the ceiling! Later on God will use this same sense of humor to reveal Himself more clearly to Job.

When criticism comes it is time to not forget to laugh, rent some Three Stooges, and read some Far Side. Somewhere I recall reading something Nietzsche supposedly said. He said a lot of stupid things in his lifetime, but he was right on this occasion. "Man alone suffers so excruciatingly in the world that he was compelled to invent laughter." There is a fourth and final way in which we can deal with hurtful criticism.

#4. Look toward home.

This is what Job did best. He kept his perspective. He knew there was more to life than just today. Look at what he said in the middle of all the criticism of round two.

> I know that my Redeemer lives, and that in the end he will stand upon the earth. And after my skin has been destroyed, yet in my flesh I will see God; I myself will see Him with my own eyes — I, and not another. How my heart yearns within me (Job 19:25-27)!

82

Job clearly sees the end. He sees the house down the lane. He views the resurrection in some way that I do not totally understand. Perhaps he didn't either. He just knew where to place his eyes. Job realized that God had prepared a place for those who love Him. Job saw it!

But I have to tell you that in the back of my mind I'm wondering why Job doesn't give in to all this criticism. Why doesn't he call a truce? Why not say, "OK guys, I know I'm not perfect. Lord, if I have sinned against you and you're punishing me for that, forgive me. I'm sorry." Wouldn't that have satisfied his buddies? I doubt it. They're good men, but they are, for the most part, legalists. It's almost as if they've been waiting offstage all these years for Job to fail. And now they can say with a hearty shout, "Gotcha! We knew you weren't as good as you let on!"

Job, though, has turned the corner in round two of conversations at the dump. He's got some things the Lord is going to show him yet. He has some straightening out that still needs tending to, but for now Job has not melted under the heat of his legalistic friends. He knows he is going to see God, his true friend, face to face — one day. It's as if Job has awaken from a horrible nightmare. Even though his friends aren't finished blasting him Job will stand strong. "I know," he says, "My redeemer lives!"

What I'm trying to say is this. All the narrow-mindedness, all the rule-keeping and all the warped theology doesn't change the Good News (John 3:16). "Whosoever" means you and me. All the criticism and harshness in the world can't change that one immutable fact.

I am a lover of good biography. Charles Spurgeon is one of my favorite people to read about. He preached in London for thirty plus years. A big man physically, he loved people and maintained a deep Christian commitment. Spurgeon, however, was not without his critics. He was criticized for a number of reasons, but nothing brought the onslaught as quickly as did his cigar smoking. He remarked how he smoked each and every cigar to the "glory of God." His critics blasted him! He responded, "When I have found intense pain relieved, a weary brain soothed, and calm, refreshing sleep obtained by a cigar, I have felt grateful to God and have blessed His name."[5] Of course, he was also criticized for his humor, for his opposition to slavery, for his relationship to the poor, for just about everything, even his preaching. Many believe, that in part, it was the strain of controversy and criticism that finally broke his health. But Spurgeon never stopped believing, "I know that my redeemer lives."

Please pay attention to this one reality. People are watching us. Some outside and even inside of the Kingdom are waiting to say, "Gotcha! I knew you were only a pretender." Criticism will come. Tragically it often comes while experiencing other kinds of suffering. Job's encouragement at the end of round two is simple: "Live a holy life, laugh a lot, love a lot and press on." Why? Because our Redeemer is seldom early, never late, but always waiting.

---

[5]Clyde E. Fant and William M. Pinson, *20 Centuries of Great Preaching*, Vol. 6 (Waco: Word, 1975 reprint), pp. 4-5. Not only are great sermons found in these volumes, but terrific biographies are present as well.

CHAPTER EIGHT

Talks At The Dump: Round Three
Job 22-31

"Never look for justice in the world, but never cease to give it. If we look for justice, we will begin to grouse and to indulge in the discontent of self-pity. . . . If we are devoted to Jesus Christ we have nothing to do with what we meet, whether it is just or unjust."[1]

I could have entitled this chapter, "How To Find God When It Hurts." I'm sure it is apparent by now that I deeply and profoundly believe that God is present at all times. The problem for me is that when suffering comes knocking at the door of my life I become so preoccupied with *me* that I miss *Him*.

There are six children in the family of John and Betty Jones, my mother and father. I have two older sisters, Kathy and Jane, both of whom work in Cincinnati, Ohio. My sisters have been salt and light in their places of employment. I am the third child, the oldest boy. I have a brother, Stephen, who is two years younger than I am. He is very bright and the linguist of the family. My second brother, Mark, lives out in Seattle, Washington. He clerks for a law firm.

Julia is my youngest sister. She was born when I was a junior in high school. It is the consensus of all my brothers

---

[1] Oswald Chambers, *My Utmost For His Highest* (Uhrichsville, OH: Barbour Books, 1991 reprint), p. 130.

and sisters, including me, that Julia got away with things that Mom and Dad never tolerated with us. We have, with delight, told her and our folks, "You would have never let us do that." "You never did that when we were young." Older children love to brag about how tough it was when they were young!

John and Betty Jones love their children. They have been good parents. They weren't always perfect and neither were their children. I certainly wasn't the model child and I have moments of profound imperfection, even now, as an adult. But they brought us up to love God and neighbor.

I tell you all of this to give some background to a story I want to share. I have been thinking about a time when there was a seventh child in our family. At least we were expecting another baby. As vividly as some memories stand out in my mind the story I'm recalling isn't as clear as I would like it to be. Somewhere between my brother, Steve, and my brother, Mark, Mom found out she was expecting another baby. We don't talk about it. Even as I write I realize that I have entered into a sacred subject. I don't recall how long Mom carried that precious baby boy, but somewhere on that wondrously mysterious road between conception and birth, he died. We have a strange word that describes that broken trip. We call it a "miscarriage." It's such a sterile word for something so deep and incomprehensible.

A number of years ago I was talking with my dad on the phone about this painful time in our family. I asked my father, "Do you remember that day?" I've asked some pretty stupid questions in my day, but that has to be one of the dumbest. I've never met a parent who didn't remember every detail of the death of one of their children. Dad's hesitancy and silence told me he recalled every painful minute. A son knows when his father is uncomfortable and doesn't want to talk. So we talked about everything else. But I remember some things about that day I need to talk about.

I remember that my two sisters and brother knew that something was wrong. A baby-sitter came to the house to watch us. That seldom happened at our home. When Mom came home from the hospital I remember looking into her face and seeing this lovely, sweet woman, crying with those silent tears that only a woman who has lost the irreplaceable can understand. She went straight to the bedroom and I don't recall anyone speaking a word the rest of the day, except in whispers. It was quiet at our house. That also seldom happened. We made our beds. We avoided fighting. We played outside. We did what we were asked to do the very first time it was asked. How ironic that the one time we all acted like civil human beings was the greatest day of sadness that I remember from my childhood. People in the church had showered Mom with gifts earlier. All of that was put away.

I never told anyone this for fear that I would be teased and misunderstood. I named the baby. I called him James Philip. I thought it sounded regal. I could call him "J.P." or I could call him "Jimmy" or "Jim." I imagined wrestling with him on the floor and teaching him "stuff" that only a big brother could teach. Though that day has long gathered dust in my memory I have quietly and humbly asked the God I love, "Where were you that day?" Most of the people I know, if they go through any kind of suffering at all, ask that question sometime. Round three of talks between Job and his three friends will take us further into our journey of looking for God in times of difficulty and pain. Let's begin by picking out the high spots of Job 22-31. We'll draw some practical conclusions before we end.

Chapter 22 comprises Eliphaz's final statement to Job. He is harsher, harder and more blunt than his previous two speeches. Eliphaz levels three accusations against Job.

1. You are a condemned man (22:1-9).
2. You are a hypocrite (22:10-20).
3. You can come back to God if you'll only repent (22:21-30).

Eliphaz, the voice of experience, the one who boldly declares, "Only the wicked suffer," offers his final answer as to why Job is suffering. Before we leave him I want you to see the charges he brings against Job. Eliphaz must bring some charges of specific sin or the theory he clings so desperately to won't hold water. For the very first time concrete accusations are leveled against the suffering man from Uz. Note them carefully.

> Is not your wickedness great? Are not your sins endless? You demand security from your brothers for no reason; you stripped men of their clothing, leaving them naked. You gave no water to the weary and you withheld food from the hungry, though you were a powerful man, owning land — an honored man, living on it. And you sent widows away empty-handed and broke the strength of the fatherless. That is why snares are all around you, why sudden peril terrifies you, why it is so dark you cannot see, and why a flood of water covers you (Job 22:5-11).

The final conclusion and obvious result of Eliphaz's charges are clear. "Job, you suffer because you are wicked." The only problem with all these accusations and all this theory is that it is false. Don't forget the opening description of Job. He was blameless, upright, feared God and shunned evil. Eliphaz wraps up his assessment in one sentence. Job has been cruel to the poor.

In chapters 23 and 24 Job offers his final rebuttal to Eliphaz. He restates his innocence, agrees that those things do happen, the poor are abused, but he (Job) has played no part in it. Chapter 25 is Bildad's final comment. Only six verses in all. He is brief, blunt and belligerent. He gets in one final harsh word on how evil man really is. Don't forget that Bildad is the voice of tradition. He is the friend who said, "The wicked always suffer." Bildad's closing words comprise two main thoughts.

1. God is holy.

2. Man is sinful.

Though Bildad means these two statements to be a surgical knife in Job's heart, he has stumbled onto something that even Job can't quite yet see. It is the truth that every person must face at some point. A person cannot stand on their own goodness alone. Being good doesn't, by itself, cut the mustard with God. In spite of Bildad's cruelty with that information he is right. Being good cannot ultimately save a person. The hardest people to talk with about a personal relationship with God, through Jesus Christ, are good, moral people. So Bildad's conclusion is clear. Job can't claim he is even good, because the wicked always suffer, not the good. The only problem with this kind of reasoning, of course, is that it too is a lie. Even good, solid-rock, morally sound people suffer. Even those who know God deeply and personally suffer.

Job's response to Bildad moves all the way from chapter 26 to 31. In chapter 26 Job sarcastically silences his friend. He offers three biting remarks. Here's the first.

1. You haven't helped me in the least bit.

This is a sample of Job's rebuttal.

> How you have helped the powerless! How you have saved the arm that is feeble! What advice you have offered to one without wisdom! And what great insight you have displayed! Who has helped you utter these words? And whose spirit spoke from your mouth? (Job 26:2-4)

In chapter 27 Job gives this counter to Bildad.

2. I still say I'm innocent.

> As long as I have life within me, the breath of God in my nostrils, my lips will not speak wickedness, and my tongue will

utter no deceit. I will never admit you are in the right; till I die, I will not deny my integrity. I will maintain my righteousness and never let go of it; my conscience will not reproach me as long as I live (Job 27:3-6).

Finally, in chapter 28, Job angrily cries.

3. You're not as smart as you think you are.

Job 28 is like a song, a hymn of wisdom with three verses.

  A. No one is smart enough to find wisdom.
  B. No one is rich enough to buy wisdom.
  C. Only God is the source of wisdom.

Job has had it with all the pain and hurt that his three friends have heaped upon him. In the final three chapters (29-31) Job recalls the past, reviews the present and restates his innocence.

First, he does what we all do when suffering comes and we can't seem to find God.

1. Job remembers "the good old days."

How I long for the months gone by, for the days when God watched over me, when his lamp shone upon my head and by his light I walked through darkness! Oh, for the days when I was in my prime, when God's intimate friendship blessed my house, when the Almighty was still with me and my children were around me, when my path was drenched with cream and the rock poured out for me streams of olive oil. When I went to the gate of the city and took my seat in the public square, the young men saw me and stepped aside and the old men rose to their feet; the chief men refrained from speaking and covered their mouths with their hands . . . (Job 29:2-9).

There's more. Listen to the precise recollections of this hurting man. He recalls honor, benevolence and blessing.

29:11 "Whoever heard of me spoke well of me."

29:15 "I was eyes to the blind and feet to the lame."

29:16 "I was a father to the needy."

29:22 "After I had spoken, they spoke no more."

Job remembers it all. He clings to the time when he was content with God, when he was famous, when he was helpful, when he was visionary. Memory after memory is brought to the surface.

In chapter 30 Job does a second thing.

2. Job rehearses "the pain of the present moment."

30:1 "They mock me, men younger than I . . . whose fathers I would have disdained to put with my sheep dogs."

30:9 "Now their sons mock me in song; I have become a byword among them."

30:10 "They detest me and keep their distance; they do not hesitate to spit in my face."

30:15 "Terrors overwhelm me; my dignity is driven away as by the wind, my safety vanishes like a cloud."

30:17 "Night pierces my bones; my gnawing pains never rest."

30:28 "I go about blackened; but not by the sun."

30:30 "My skin grows black and peels; my body burns with fever."

There is the present for Job! All that he is experiencing is an absolute nightmare!

Chapter 31 is Job's final claim of innocence to his three friends. Here he drives his deepest stake. He lays claim to being not guilty of all the charges. Sixteen times Job repeats himself with the phrase, "If I have," "If my heart," or "If my steps." 31:5,6 set the mood of the whole section.

If I have walked in falsehood or my foot has hurried after deceit — let God weigh me in honest scales and he will know that I am blameless.

91

What I want us to see after all is said and done ("The words of Job are ended.") is that there is still no resolution. We find Job on one side claiming his innocence and his friends on the other side pronouncing his guilt. They are locked in a stalemate. All of it seems so clear to Zophar that he doesn't even bother to speak in the final round of talks at the dump. But may I remind all of us that this stalemate is not just between Job and company, but also between Job and God. Job cries out. God remains silent. Too much talk can sink a friendship. Too much talk can blossom into ugly criticism. Too much talk can cloud the presence of God!

How does a person find God when suffering appears to close the door on the presence of God? Where is God when we feel like our prayers are bouncing off the ceiling? C. S. Lewis grappled with these questions. While grieving over the loss of his wife, Joy, he asked some difficult questions.

> Meanwhile, where is God? This is one of the most disquieting symptoms. When you are happy, so happy that you have no sense of needing Him, so happy that you are tempted to feel His claims upon you as an interruption, if you remember yourself and turn to Him with gratitude and praise, you will be — or so it feels — welcomed with open arms. But go to Him when your need is desperate, when all other help is vain, and what do you find? A door slammed in your face and a sound of bolting and double bolting on the inside. After that, silence. You may as well turn away. The longer you wait, the more emphatic the silence will become. . . . What does this mean? Why is He so present a commander in our time of prosperity and so very absent a help in time of trouble?[2]

Lewis does work through his pain. He gets through the hurt, anger and confusion and eventually writes some of the most insightful material ever on pain and suffering. But in the mean time he asked, "Where is God?" "How do I find Him?"

------

[2]Lewis, *A Grief Observed*, pp. 4-5.

In closing out the third round of talks I thought it would be helpful if I could offer some practical suggestions in locating God in the fog of our heartache. I jotted down six helps that I have watched others implement, that I have implemented.

#1. Admit helplessness.

Job did that. When we stop trying to fix things on our own then God can often do his best work. Job finally shoves all his goodness aside and allows God to be God. We'll see this more clearly later.

#2. Face anger.

I would like for all of us to be free from the tyranny of thinking that we have to be so under control. The Psalms are filled with examples of the writer admitting what burns within his heart. So much of suffering seems unfair. If we could just confess that we are mad and upset some of the mist might begin to blow away.

#3. Commit time.

I'm talking about getting into the Scriptures at this point. I have watched people who knew little about God come to a place like the Psalms and find God and comfort. Apparently Job came back to some form of the Scriptures. He makes this remarkable statement.

"I have not departed from the commands of his lips; I have treasured the words of his mouth more than my daily bread" (23:12).

Some of you can share firsthand how you found God in the Bible when you were going through a horrible season of suffering.

93

#4. Invest service.

What I mean is, if it is physically possible, start to help someone else. Take your eyes and attention off of yourself. Everybody has heard of Joni Eareckson Tada, who was paralyzed from a swimming accident in 1967. In her own words she proclaims this truth. "My need for help is obvious every day when I wake up, flat on my back, waiting for someone to come dress me. I can't even comb my hair or blow my nose alone."[3] Most of you also know what she has accomplished by the grace of God. After deep despair and wide barriers Joni has invested her life in other people. She paints some of the most beautiful pictures, with her teeth, and now travels all over speaking, writing and encouraging others. In her own words, "Okay, I'm paralyzed. It's terrible. I don't like it. But can God still use me, paralyzed? Can I, paralyzed, still worship God and love Him? He has taught me I can."[4]

#5. Wait patiently.

This one is so hard. Sometimes a person feels like they've been cheated when bad things happen. They feel they did nothing to deserve their current crisis. They may be right. I only know that the people who have found God in their situation are those who have viewed their suffering as a temporary delay. That's as tough as nails, but so essential. Christians really are pilgrims in progress.

#6. Accept God as Lord.

This one is the most obvious and the most needed.

---

[3]Phil Yancey, *Where Is God When It Hurts?*, p. 111. Yancey may very well be one of the finest contemporary writers on the subject of suffering. His works are highly acclaimed.

[4]Ibid., p. 119.

Everything else is secondary. God is not just Lord of the good times. Those who find Him are the ones who see that He is God of all the times, good and bad. He is their Lord regardless of what happens or doesn't happen.

So where is God? How do we find Him when it hurts so much that we can hardly get out of bed? In any church, any fellowship, there are people on the outside who constantly call on her to lend a helping hand. When I was pastoring a local congregation there was a woman who just kept calling and calling. She always lived in crisis, always needed something. She was terribly difficult to talk to. You had to explain things to her six or seven times. She had a speech impediment which made it difficult for me to understand her. We'll call her Patricia.

Miss Patricia called me around Thanksgiving one year. She was worried that the church would forget about her need. I repeated over and over that the food would be coming to the front door of her house. If I said it once I said it a dozen times, "Patricia, the food will be coming to your front door." In my zealous repetition a memory was triggered in my mind that I had not considered for a long time. It was a story that a friend of mine had once told me.

I imagined that I was Patricia, which in some way that I cannot explain to you, I am. I suppose we all are. I was on a journey and I came to the top of a hill overlooking a town. I wasn't sure where to go and how to find things so I looked for the steeple of a church, but I couldn't find one. I stopped to ask, "Where's the steeple? I need to find a church." Everyone I spoke with said the same thing, "I don't know. I've never seen one. I guess we don't need one."

I walked further into town, clean streets, lovely boulevards, beautiful trees, manicured lawns. I saw some roses so I bent over and admired them. I said to someone walking by, "Why, these roses don't have any thorns. Where are they?" "I don't know," she said, "We don't need them here."

I strolled downtown and I noticed there weren't any locks on the doors, no hospitals, no counseling centers, no social agencies, no police stations. Everyone I stopped said the same thing, "We don't need them here." I came to the center of town. What I saw there I could not believe. I rubbed my eyes and stared in absolute amazement. I saw my brother, James Philip. I don't know how I knew it was him, I just did. He smiled. There at his side was the Lamb, the King of Kings and Lord of Lords. And I started to cry. James Philip said, "We don't need that here." Suddenly everything made sense. Everything. My imagination brought me home again and Patricia didn't seem so bothersome anymore.

Round three has ended. It is important to remind myself and you that "God will always tax the fullest resources of infinite minds and tongues and still leave men wondering, pondering and adoring."[5] God waits for just the right time to enter and reveal His presence. After all, it wouldn't be proper to barge in on something as holy as preparation for heaven. As far as I know, He is seldom early, but never late.

---

[5]Robert Drummond, *Faith's Perplexities* (New York: American Tract Society, n.d.), pp. 283-285.

CHAPTER NINE

What Friends Are For
Job 32-37

"Tell me what your conception of God is and I will work out your doctrine of man, of forgiveness, of life, of punishment. . . . The chief service of a prophet is not to rebuke sin, nor instruct in virtue; it is to give the world a radiant idea of God. . . ."[1]

Carole Sager and Burt Bacharach composed a song about the purpose of friends. I don't recall all the words, but I do remember these few lines.

"Keep smiling. Keep shining,
knowing you can always count on me.
For sure, that's what friends are for.
For good times and bad times,
I'll be on your side forevermore —
for sure — that's what friends are for."

I first understood the nature of friendship from Mark Donovan. He was a childhood buddy. He had the blondest hair of any boy in town. Some of us called him "Whitey." Mark was an only child who happened to have more toys than any kid I knew at the time. Every week he got fifty cents

---

[1]John Watson, *Mind of the Master* (New York: Dodd, Mead & Co., 1896), found in W.A. Pratney's, *The Nature and Character of God* (Minneapolis: Bethany House, 1988), p. 14. I highly recommend Pratney's work for reflection and digestion.

for his allowance. I thought he must have been the richest kid around. We spent a great deal of time together playing out in his backyard. When we played "army" he always wanted me to be the first one to die. Mark never wanted to die, so I always surrendered my life on the battlefield. I got pretty good at it. I could die for five minutes after a fatal wound! If there had been a crowd around to watch my grand performance I'm sure they would have awarded me with a standing ovation and an "Oscar." Mark shared everything he had with me. Every Saturday morning, like clockwork, we would celebrate our friendship with his fifty cents down at the local drugstore. He would buy us each a penny pretzel and a nickel coke. I recall his companionship with great affection. That's what friends are for.

We eventually moved away from that central Illinois town and I found new friends in southwestern Pennsylvania. Meet Alan Hill and Ronnie Hart. Alan was a very good friend. I loved the silver tooth he had in the middle of his front teeth. It was as shiny as a new faucet. Not many kids have something that wonderful in their mouth! What a great conversation starter! Alan was always ready to play anything: kickball, baseball, or football. We would play for hours and then go get a bottle of pop down at Howell's neighborhood grocery. We'd talk and laugh. That's what friends are for.

Ronnie Hart was as wide as he was tall, with a heart as big as the great outdoors. I mentioned him in a previous chapter. I remember one night we stayed down at his house and put together a model of PT-109. We decided to stay up all night. We listened to Alan Funk records, laughed ourselves silly, and stuffed our bellies with cookies and bologna sandwiches. We drank down 16 ounce bottles of Mello-Yellow and Tab! When morning came I blessed his front porch with all the goodies of the previous night's party. Even that only deepened our friendship. I guess that's what friends are for.

Several years later my dad was called to a church in north-central Indiana. I met John Garrett there and we played hours of basketball together. When I first encountered John in the seventh grade we were about the same height. By the time we were sophomores in High School he was over 6'5" and when he went off to play basketball at Purdue University he was a seven-footer. He even made the front cover of *Sports Illustrated* as Indiana's "Mr. Basketball!" We used to "cruise" in his Mustang, play basketball at Maconaqua Park and guzzle down quarts of root beer at the Dog-N-Suds. Sometimes we would go out to the local Air Force base and play ball with some of the airmen.

One summer we played in a basketball league together. We didn't lose a single game. We dreamed of stardom. Though he was the only one with real talent, he never laughed at my hope of one day playing for the Celtics! Having a friend that you can share your wildest and craziest ideas with and not be ridiculed, surely is a gift from God. Isn't that what friends are for? We moved away from there several years later back to Illinois. There I met Jim and Dan Harper, brothers, who have remained my lifetime friends. Writing about their friendship would entail a book all by itself.

The Bible is filled with great friendships. There is Moses and Joshua, Elijah and Elisha, Jonathan and David, Paul and Barnabas, and Jesus and the Twelve. Jerry and Mary White are absolutely correct. In their book, *Friends and Friendship*, they observe, "No one can have a meaningful existence without love and friendship. They are the substance of our emotional life."[2]

There is a rare friendship recorded in the book of Job. It is probably one of the most overlooked and least known friendships in the whole Bible. It is rare, not because it's any

---

[2]Jerry and Mary White, *Friends*, p. 10.

more special than other friendships, but because it allows us to peek into a side of friendship that is so unique. The side of friendship I'm referring to is the tough side, the side that cares enough to confront a friend. The writer of Proverbs understood this. "Better is open rebuke than hidden love. Wounds from a friend can be trusted" (Prov. 27:5,6). In our reflection from Job we have observed the relationship that existed between Job, Eliphaz, Bildad and Zophar, but all along there has been a fourth friend waiting offstage. His name is Elihu. He appears a lot younger than Job's other three friends, which is perfectly fine. Being the same age has never been a prerequisite for a rich friendship. Job 32:4ff gives us a little background.

32:4 "Elihu had waited before speaking to Job because they were older than he."

32:6 "I am young in years, and you are old; that is why I was fearful, not daring to tell you what I know."

32:7 "I thought, 'Age should speak; advanced years should teach wisdom.'"

32:8 "It is the spirit in a man, the breath of the Almighty, that gives him understanding."

32:9 "It is not only the old who are wise, not only the aged who understand what is right."

Elihu can't stand it any longer. He has had enough of the conversation at the dump for two primary reasons.

1. He believes Job isn't seeing the whole thing clearly.
2. Elihu is convinced Job's three friends haven't helped one bit. The only thing they have accomplished is to condemn Job and make him feel worse.

All of chapter 32 is devoted to Elihu's frustration with the entire dialogue between Job and the three friends. Through Elihu we get an extraordinary glimpse into a biblical friendship.

Over the years I have been blessed with lots of acquaintances, some of those have become friends. A handful have become intimate friends. But I never had a friend who said to me, "J.K., what you said, what you did, was not quite right. You were wrong. I'm going to risk our friendship to tell you that." I was almost twenty years old before I had a friend who stood up to me in love.

With courage, compassion, carefulness and a willingness to confront, Elihu, the true friend, enters the story. I want to carve out of these chapters (32-37), where Elihu speaks, six ingredients that help us to grasp the true meaning of friendship. Elihu models these six in front of a suffering friend. It is important for me to tell you that not all of the commentators who write and reflect on Job agree with me that Elihu really did anything worthy of attention. Some biblical scholars see nothing new in Elihu's words. Some even believe Elihu's speech to be an interpolation. That's a fancy way of saying that someone came along later and inserted this section. Some unknown person added material that was not an original part of the text or narrative.

Some folks are convinced that the story of Job moves naturally from chapter 31, Job's final words to his friends, to chapter 38, where the Lord enters the drama and speaks. And I admit that they have some good arguments for their reasoning. However, Elihu adds a deeper dimension to the story. From my humble vantage point there is not enough evidence for me to argue with those who fail to see Elihu as part of the original story. Since I am convinced that Elihu was a part of the original narrative let's simply observe what this fourth counselor brings to the drama. Let's start with the most obvious characteristic of a friend.

#1. Friends make good sounding boards.

Listening. Elihu had kept his mouth shut for days. He had earned the right to speak. He was a true sounding board. I want you to pay attention to what he says to Job and to the three friends.

> I waited while you spoke, I listened to your reasoning; while you were searching for words, I gave you my full attention. But not one of you have proved Job wrong; none of you has answered his arguments (32:11-12).

Did you notice that phrase, "full attention?" Job had a friend who really tuned into what was being said. Elihu is saying, "I understood, I perceived clearly what was being said. I observed it all. I discerned everything." The Hebrew word used here is a word that indicates "knowledge." It is a knowledge which is superior to just gathering the facts. Elihu sorted it all out and he knew what to do with what he found. That's what friends are for. They are supposed to fully give attention, to sort out what we say and then know what to do with it. True biblical friendship is like that.

If you zero in on 32:11 you can see a great model for listening. Notice how the scene unfolds.

A. Elihu allows everyone else to speak first.
B. He followed the course of what was being said.
C. He did not interrupt.
D. He gave his undivided attention to the entire matter.

Friends do that. Let's build on this first ingredient.

#2. Friends meet us eye to eye.

Real friends meet us at our level. They identify with us. This is what Elihu models in the first portion of chapter 33.

> Answer me then, if you can; prepare yourself and confront me. I am just like you before God; I too have been taken from clay. No fear of me should alarm you, nor should my hand be heavy upon you (33:5-7).

Isn't that refreshing? There is a huge difference between Elihu, the friend, and the other three companions. Elihu confessed his own humanness. True friendships grow under that kind of roof. This young man is accepting Job right where he is, just as he is.

Acceptance is an intricate part of friendship. Every person I ever met is flawed in some way. Every person at some point reveals they are made of clay. What friends are for has nothing to do with perfection, but has a whole lot to do with acceptance and identification.

Let's build even further.

#3. Friends care enough to take us seriously.

At the end of chapter 33 we read these words. Observe what Elihu asks of Job that the other three friends failed to ask.

> If you have anything to say, answer me; speak up, for I want you to be cleared. But if not, then listen to me; be silent, and I will teach you wisdom (33:32-33).

The clincher is that Elihu wanted Job to be "cleared." He wanted his friend to be justified, to be right with God and people again. In the larger context what Elihu is saying is something like this.

"Job, I want you to be the one who serves God and helps the blind, the lame, the poor and the hurting again. I want that for you." To take someone seriously enough to care about them is the grand and glorious potential of God-centered friendships.

Imagine someone leaving the church building one morning after Sunday service. She hangs up her robe hastily in the choir room while muttering under her breath, "I quit." You're sure she is kidding. This person always jokes around, so you respond, "Me too." "No," she says, "I mean it! I quit." You ask her, "What's wrong?" "No one takes me seriously," she responds. You aren't sure what to say, except, "What would it take to get you to change your mind?" Out it comes. What this one person, in one church has longed for her whole life. "I need someone to take me seriously." People would rather fight than be snubbed. Elihu cared. He showed courage. He took Job seriously. Even in all the sarcasm of Job's pain, Elihu took his friend seriously.

I read through Bill Hybels' small, but mighty book, *Who You Are When No One's Looking*. I loved what he said in his chapter on courage.

> It . . . takes relational courage to build significant relationships with friends, to look another person in the eye, and say, "Isn't it time we stopped talking about the weather and the stock market and started talking about what's going on in your life and mine. Isn't it time we became brothers?" Not many (people) have the courage to challenge each other, to fight for each other's spiritual and relational growth.[3]

That's what friends are for. Biblical friends have a mandate from God to take each other seriously, to care with grace and firmness. Here's another ingredient.

#4. Friends remind us of what we tend to forget.

It's more than appointments, dates and commitments I'm talking about here. Remember that Job is suffering enormously. Friends are supposed to remind us of two great truths when pain comes knocking.

1. Friends are supposed to remind us that God speaks in our suffering. He is not silent and indifferent.

---

[3]Bill Hybels, *Who You Are When No One's Looking* (Downers Grove: InterVarsity, 1987), p. 18.

2. Friends are supposed to remind us that God has a wise and good plan even in the most dire of circumstances.

This is what Elihu tells Job on several occasions. Here is an example. "For God does speak, now one way, now another — though man may not perceive it" (33:14). What Job couldn't believe was that God had a purpose in all this madness. Elihu challenges him to rethink his worldview. He tells Job to forget the righteous vs unrighteous issue. "Look at God. He's got something to say. You're fighting against that, Job." Our list of ingredients are closing fast. Here's the fifth one.

#5. Friends set us straight when necessary.

I love those lines, even though they hurt, in 33:12. Elihu tells Job what only a true friend can. Job has been complaining at length about how God has not understood him. Elihu says, as a surgical friend, "But I tell you, in this you are not right." God is not Job's enemy. Now there's a friend! Do you have a friend like that? I have only a few people in my life who have earned the right to say that to me. "J.K., in this you are not right." I return to the Whites and their book on friendship. Jerry offers a humble reminder.

> I once noticed a problem area in a friend but sensed no freedom to pursue it. Instead I prayed for about a year. Then one day he brought the issue up himself and opened the door for me to share my observations. Friendship is not a hunting license for special weaknesses. When correction occurs, however, this exchange between close friends will strengthen rather than threaten an already strong friendship. There is assurance in knowing that a friend will help us grow and develop. The Holy Spirit corrects us daily, but we may not be sensitive to that correction. So the Spirit may choose to use a friend to point out the error.[4]

---

[4]Jerry and Mary White, *Friends*, p. 79.

Amen. That's what friends are for. Here's the final ingredient on our list.

#6. Friends encourage us with the "Big Picture."

Job 37 is all about the "Big Picture." Read the first few verses and see what I mean.

> At this my heart pounds and leaps from its place. Listen! Listen to the roar of his voice, to the rumbling that comes from his mouth. He unleashes his lightning beneath the whole heaven and sends it to the ends of the earth. After that comes the sound of his roar; he thunders with his majestic voice. When his voice resounds, he holds nothing back. God's voice thunders in marvelous ways; he does great things beyond our understanding. He says to the snow, "Fall on the earth," and to the rain shower, "Be a mighty downpour" (37:1-6).

The "Big Picture" is that God is Lord over everything: lightning, thunder, snow, rain and the implication in the context is that God is even Lord over suffering. As Creator and Redeemer all things are subject to Him. I want you to look at one small verse in chapter 37 with me. Elihu tries to explain why people suffer. It's not a complete list of reasons, but it seems to help Job. Elihu uses an agricultural picture. In speaking of God, he says, "He brings the clouds to punish men, or to water his earth and show his love" (37:13). Do you see the point? The clouds are an analogy of suffering. God allows suffering for at least three reasons according to Elihu.

1. Sometimes God allows suffering in order to correct those who go astray. Like rain does to those who think they control the earth.
2. Sometimes God allows suffering in order to rescue us and strengthen our faith. Like rain does for dry land. Rain rescues the earth from drought.

3. Sometimes God allows suffering in order to test the loyalty of those who say they love God.

In Hebrew the word for "love" used here is mercy. Mercy is the act of God that spares us from not getting what we deserve. In the agricultural analogy we deserve no rain, but we get abundant rain as needed. In Job's plight, no matter how good he thinks he is, he doesn't deserve anything good, but God gives it out of love. It is a huge and complicated picture being presented by Elihu, the true friend. Elihu passionately wants Job to realize that God's ownership and Lordship is extended over everything, including Job.

If we tied all these ingredients together and put them in one little package we could say, "Friends are for preparing us to meet God." That, my dear reader, is not small potatoes! Friendship is to be a rehearsal prior to spending eternity with God, our Great and Glorious Friend! Immediately after Elihu finishes his speech God enters the drama. Job is so touched by it all he doesn't speak a single word, not one.

True biblical friends bring us closer to God. They move us deeper and deeper into a personal relationship with Christ. This is what we want, all of us, and don't know it. To think that I almost missed it myself scares me to death. I was about twenty years old and working in a tire shop in Marshall, Illinois. I daily changed and repaired passenger, truck and tractor tires. It's the kind of work, I imagine, people will do who don't enter into heaven. I remember my hands were cut and sore from handling the calcium chloride and pinching my fingers in the rims of the tires. I confess that I was bitter because I had to drop out of college due to the lack of money. My heart hurt worse than my blistered hands. I was down on the church and down on people. I compromised my love for Christ repeatedly. I was a prodigal. I was mad at the world and mad at no one in particular.

One day a local farmer, who shall remain nameless, came

into the tire store with a flat combine tire. He began to boss everyone around. He had an opinion about everything and only his opinion was right. He commenced to explain to me how to correctly repair a combine tire. It was the third time that he said, "I'd do it this way, if I were you," that set me off. I swore at him, picked up the nearest object I could find, which was a tire tool and threw it at him. "Since you know so much about it you fix it yourself!" I couldn't believe what was happening. All of the poison coming out of me. Fortunately for me the farmer ducked and my boss, Dan Harper, was more gracious than I was.

Sometimes I see people who remind me of what I was like back then. They are searching, bitter, blaming and hurting, just like I was and just like Job was. Do you know what turned it around for me? I wish I could tell you that I did it on my own. I wish I could say that I started reading the Scriptures and I read my way out of the mess. I wish I could say I walked across America and found God, but I can't say any of those things. I'll tell you how it happened.

I was on my way to Champaign, Illinois in order to take Jim Harper, Dan's oldest son, back to the university. Jim asked me to drive so that he could talk with me about some things he needed to get "off his chest." Somewhere between Marshall and Champaign Jim became my Elihu. "John, you know I love you. You are my friend. But you are driving everyone away. You're bitter and you've blamed everyone, but yourself. Maybe it is nobody's fault. You need to make a choice to live fully or to die."

I couldn't believe what I was hearing. I didn't say a word. Jim was right. It took about four years of God using the Navigator's ministry and military service to bring me around, but that day with Jim was my turning point. The great mystery in Job's story is that when Elihu finishes talking Job is ready to begin his life anew. God is on the way and it was all ushered in because of a friend. One of the most magnificent and most overlooked tools in bringing people to God through Christ is friendship. The good news is, anybody can do it. That's what friends are for, especially when one of those friends is suffering. Wherever a true friend exists God will seldom be early, but never, never late.

CHAPTER TEN

What Is God Saying To Us?
Job 38-41

"To trust the Origin of our existence is the fundamental grace of life. Every virtue, every grace possible to the soul, must be the outcome of that fundamental trust. . . . The fidelity of God is that adorable perfection in His nature upon which everything in the universe lies down to rest. Our blessed Creator refers to His faithfulness that His creatures have to deal with more constantly and more universally than any other one attribute of His nature . . . ."[1]

In talking about life, that great English preacher, Martin Lloyd-Jones, once said, "There is a mystery about it which you cannot get at. . . . There is something else after all, beyond, above, behind all we can understand."[2] Mystery. There were some things in my growing up years that I counted as unexplainable. Falling stars mystified me. Sometimes I would get up from bed in the middle of the night while everyone else was asleep and sit at the window in my bedroom and watch. And maybe I would see a star falling, there it was, just for a split second. The kids on the block

---

[1]W.A. Pratney, *Nature and Character of God*, pp. 190-191. This is a quote from George Watson, "Necessity of Trusting God," in *Our Own God*, pp. 150-151. I have been greatly blessed by Pratney's devotional apologetic on the nature and character of God. I highly recommend it.

[2]Fant and Pinson, *20 Centuries of Great Preaching*, "Lloyd Jones," Vol. XI, p. 293.

where I lived used to say, "When a star falls it means that a witch has died somewhere." I found comfort in that, but it was all a mystery to me. I imagined that a falling star was just a white pebble that got skipped across the dark sky by God. I used to skip flat stones across the dark water at Jack Seller's gravel pit when I was a boy. I reasoned if I received such great pleasure from skipping things maybe God did too.

Birth was always a grand mystery to me. How people were born, how they ended up in a certain family, rather than in another gave me hours of contemplation. I found the idea of birth fascinating. Kids talked about the stork making deliveries, or there being this special place where babies waited until someone called their number. Then they were dropped down this heavenly chute something like the fire escape at the local grade school. Some of my friends thought that the whole process of birth and placement was all left up to chance. Sometimes we would tease each other with statements like, "You don't really belong in your family. Your parents found you. Nobody wanted you. Your mom and dad felt sorry for you and took you in."

Of course, none of that helped to explain the mystery. I recall a time when I found a litter of newly born kittens out in the rose bushes in our backyard. Some mother cat had apparently abandoned her children just after their birth. I marveled at these little creatures with such small whimpers. Their eyes were closed and they seemed so helpless. "How did it all happen?" I wondered. I cleaned them up and got them something to eat, some milk and some chocolate cake! What did I know? It was all beyond comprehension for me.

I thought about the flight of birds. If birds can fly I wondered why I couldn't? I thought I was as smart as a bird. Surely I could figure this one out. I studied their flight and read what the encyclopedia had to say about birds and flight. I fashioned wings out of some old rackets and cloth and I sailed off of a neighbor's shed. It was a mystery that I lived!

112

Mysteries were all around me. I wondered why people sneezed? How did I end up with this thing called an Adam's apple? Why couldn't I hold my breath longer than I did? How did worms get inside of apples? How did birds learn to build such nice homes? Why were stars able to twinkle? How did God end up with the offering on Sunday mornings? I was told the offering was for Him. How did He get it? Did He come down Himself and sneak into the auditorium when no one was around? Did He send an angel? Mysteries. Yet, most of what I considered a mystery then has become explainable, at least a little. I learned about stars, the human body and creatures of the world and I keep most of that information filed away in the back of my mind when my children ask me questions that I once asked. But, for me, there is always the unexplainable mystery of suffering that I just can't seem to get past.

We are in a section of our reflection from Job that almost kept me from writing this book. We now enter into the portion of the story where God finally speaks, where Job finally gets what he has been asking for all along. Job gets a personal interview with God. At last Job gets to defend himself. He finally gets an opportunity to be acquitted. However, we could entitle these next few chapters of Job, "Be Careful What You Ask For." Or we could call it, "Thank God He Doesn't Always Give Us What We Want." There is mystery all over this part of the drama. God is going to give Job a "Pop Science" quiz, which, of course, Job will fail miserably. What I would like to do is simply mark out three questions that come to all of us when we begin to feel and believe that God isn't in control of what's happening around us. The first question comes from the first twenty-one verses of Job 38.

#1. *"Do you know how I made the earth?"*

That's God's first question to Job. The question doesn't seem to fit the question we have been pursuing, the same question Job and all of his companions have been pursuing, "Why is Job suffering? Why do we suffer?" In 38:1 God comes to Job out of a storm, or a whirlwind. Without introduction or fanfare God begins to grill Job.

> Who is this that darkens my counsel with words without knowledge? Brace yourself like a man; I will question you, and you shall answer me. Where were you when I laid the earth's foundation? Tell me, if you understand" (Job 38:2-4).

A whole onslaught of questions about creation follow. Here is a small portion.

38:12 "Have you ever given orders to the morning, or shown the dawn its place?"

38:17 "Have the gates of death been shown to you?"

38:19 "What is the way to the abode of light? And where does darkness reside?"

38:21 "Surely you know, for you were already born! You have lived so many years!"

God asks Job face to face, "Do you know how I made the earth?"

It doesn't seem fair, does it? Job only wants to get his question answered, "Why am I suffering?" All God wants to talk about is the mystery of creation. What is God trying to say? Hold that thought and consider this second question.

#2. *"Do you know how I keep the universe running?"*

God's response to His own question runs from 38:22 to 39:30. In this large section God tests Job about snow and hail, lightning and rain, ice and frost, stars and clouds, the mind and the heart. He interrogates Job about ten different kinds of animals. It's all overwhelming for the man from Uz. I offer a simple paraphrase.

38:39 "Job, what do you know about lions?"

38:41 "Job, what do you know about ravens?"

114

39:1 "What do you know about mountain lions?"

39:2 "What do you know about deer?"

39:5 "Tell me everything you know about wild donkey?"

39:9 "What research have you done on the wild ox?"

39:13 "How about the ostrich? I didn't bless her with a great deal of sense, but she can run like the wind. What do you know about that?"

39:19 "Tell me what you know about the horse?"

39:26 "Give me your insight into the hawk or the eagle."

Every animal God mentions in His oral exam of Job is unique. Each one has gifts and flaws, pluses and minuses, grace and handicaps. The whole thing is a mystery. Question after question after question. No answers. Questions only. It feels like Job asks for a fish and God gives him a snake. Job simply asks for an egg and God gives him a scorpion.

God wants Job to explain and share his understanding on how the world was created and how it continues to function. All Job wants is the answer to his crisis. Job wants to know why.

"Why did my kids have to die?

Why did I lose everything I held as valuable?

Why am I sitting out here in this dump, on this pile of burnt manure and trash?

Why is my body no longer recognizable?

Why is this happening to me?"

Anybody who is a student of the Scriptures or has experienced much of life knows that God could change it all instantly. God could say, "I think I'll heal Job. It would be easier than explaining it all to him." A person might think that God has made His point with Job. Not so! At the beginning of chapter 40 a new quiz begins. God gives Job a chance to respond, But Job squeaks out only three sentences.

I am unworthy — how can I reply to you? I put my hand over my mouth. I spoke once, but I have no answer — twice, but I will say no more (Job 40:4-5).

115

Then comes the third and final question. Here is the question all of us are asked when we begin to think that God isn't in charge any longer.

#3. "Do you know what you would keep and what you would throw away in the world?"

God uses two illustrations in questioning Job at this point. In chapter 40 the Lord speaks of the behemoth or as most have taught, the hippopotamus. In chapter 41 God uses the leviathan or probably the crocodile in His examination of Job. It is possible (some think probable) that both these references are to dinosaurs. We could entitle chapters 40 and 41, "Everything You Always Wanted To Know About Hippos, Crocodiles, or Dinosaurs, But Were Afraid To Ask!" There is such profound and infinite detail provided by God as he unfolds question after question to Job. God speaks of the weirdest animal on land and the wildest one in water. Both animals can live in water or land, both are feared. Again, The Lord overwhelms Job with a flood of questions. "Job, do you know why I made them? Can anyone control them, except me?" The Creator of the universe uses these two weird and wild creatures to ask His biggest question. "Job, what would you keep and what would you throw away if you were left in charge of it all?" Listen to what God is really asking.

40:8-14 "Job, would you keep the wicked or throw them out?"
40:15-24 "Job, would you keep the useless or throw them out?"
41:1-34 "Job, would you keep the hostile or throw them out?"

Yet, all Job wants to know is, "Why is this happening to me?" And God doesn't offer one word about Job's suffering. There are no brilliant words or explanation from God on the theology of evil. God doesn't even answer the charges Job brought concerning injustices: the good suffering and the evil skating along through life. Instead of answering questions, God asks them! Does that make sense? God ignores all of

Job's concerns and instead focuses all His unlimited energy on His creative power and on His wise, benevolent Lordship. Why? It is the grandest mystery I know. Why?

There is a tough side of God. Lots of folks can't take this side of God. As much as I have appreciated Rabbi Harold Kushner's book, *When Bad Things Happen To Good People*, it is quite clear that Kushner cannot accept this God of mystery. Please hear me. To believe in God is to believe in mystery! I have watched people (and you have too) come and go in the Christian life. They want everything spelled out clearly in sweet little packages. They want teachings and sermons on tithing, sinfulness, baptism or evangelism, because they think all those things are black and white. But there is huge mystery behind all those subjects too! The crime of Job's three friends was not their insensitivity to Job, but their incredible insensitivity toward God. They explained everything away.

I keep asking myself, "What are we going to do as Christians after we have an answer for everything? What will we do after we put a label and title on every piece of suffering? What will we do then?" As long as I am asking questions here is another one. Why doesn't God just answer Job? Get it over with. Give Job the missing piece to the puzzle. Here is my brilliant response, "I don't know." In Phil Yancey's book, *Where Is God When It Hurts?*, he offers this explanation to our key question.

> God wants us to freely choose to love Him, even when that choice involves pain — because we are committed to Him, not to our own good feelings and rewards. He wants us to cleave to Him, as Job did, even when we have every reason to hotly deny Him.[3]

I don't know if I am right or not, but I believe Job 38-41 is

---

[3]Yancey, *Where Is God When It Hurts?*, p. 69.

all about one mysterious thing. These monumental chapters are about God's Lordship over all of life. God, in all those seventy plus questions to Job, is talking about His sovereign control, even when things do not make sense. That one idea is so difficult to embrace for our "microwave" generation. What I am talking about here is a surrendering of our possessions, our relationships, our dreams. God is saying one simple, amazing, colossal statement. Are you beginning to hear it?

Faith doesn't come after a big pile of proof is dumped on our lap. Faith is never conjured up after all our "whys" are answered. The single, most mysterious subject for me in the Christian life is that God keeps talking about "Who," not "Why."

I wish with all my heart that I could make this section of Job clearer. I know that some of you have deep, painful "whys" you long to be answered. I believe with all my heart that God is in control. God does care. Our Father in heaven is consistent. Go back with me to Job 40:8. God asks, "Would you discredit my justice? Would you condemn me to justify yourself?" The Lord seems to admit that there are times and places when things *appear* to be out of control, yet these are areas He rules and reigns as supreme commander. God declares, "Everything under heaven belongs to me" (41:11). I wonder what God is trying to say to us?

December 26, 1973, one day after Christmas, I was guarding a string of KC-135 Tankers for the United States Air Force. There was a foot of snow on the ground and the temperature was 15 below zero. I was alone and for the first time in my life I truly missed home. The only person I saw during the entire eight hour shift of duty was an old staff sergeant who would occasionally come around in his warm vehicle and ask me if I was cold! I was so down that I recall going over to the wheel of one of those large jets and leaning against it as if that was the only thing left for me to do.

I started to cry one of those cleansing cries. Of course, the tears froze on my cheeks. For the first time in a long time, I prayed. I needed some kind of answer and I'm not even sure if I knew what the question was. I couldn't see one good thing in my entry into the military. Two months later I met the Navigators on that base! Maybe that doesn't mean anything to you, but it was a literal life-saver for me. All along God was teaching me about His Lordship, about waiting, about character building. God was answering "Who" and I was asking "Why."

People often give me items they have made. A longtime friend of mine gave me a counted-cross stitch of Psalm 90:12, "Teach us to number our days aright that we may gain a heart of wisdom." Have you ever taken a good look at pictures made out of cross-stitch? I'm not talking about the front of the picture, but I'm referring to the backside of the frame. If you peel back the protective paper that usually covers the back portion you'll discover that there are lines of thread going every which way. It's a mess. When you take a good look at the backside all the threads and colors seem to have a purposeless direction. However, when you sneak a peek at the front side every strand, every thread, every color, every stitch forms a beautiful creation. The front side makes everything clear. Do you hear what I'm saying? The longer a person walks with God the closer that person gets to seeing the front side. It's a tough journey, because so often on the trip we only get to see the back side. The back side doesn't seem to make any sense at all.

The grand and glorious good news is this. A simple act of faith opens up the possibility of one day seeing the front side of God's purpose. Do you hear what God is saying to us in Job 38-41? God is declaring to all of us who live our lives quietly enough so that we can hear Him, "Trust me. Trust me. I am seldom early, but believe me when I say, I am never late for you."

119

CHAPTER ELEVEN
After Suffering Come the Gifts
Job 42:1-6

"There is no book of Job in the New Testament. . . . Two things strike us with surprise there. First of all, we are struck by the fact that Christ's attitude toward suffering is so different from that of others. And secondly, one is shocked by the fact that so few Christians have adopted Jesus' attitude toward suffering."[1]

The single most difficult thing to believe about suffering is that it is the back door through which God can bless us deeply and richly. I am a sports enthusiast. That's a nice way of saying that if I'm not careful I could spend my days drinking down large jugs of basketball, football, baseball and whatever else I can get my hands on! I have an addiction. I was never a great athlete, but I always loved to participate. The first organized sport I ever played in was Little League Baseball. I was a member, in good standing, of the Heyworth White Sox. Mr. O'Neil was our coach. I think there must have been a shortage of eligible boys that year (pre-girl era), because I was drafted at the age of nine when the age of eligibility was 10-12. It didn't matter to me how I got to play. The only thing I cared about was playing.

Coach O'Neil decided to have me try out at first base. It was about the time when Mickey Mantle moved from the outfield for the Yankees and began to play first base. It didn't

---

[1]Jones, *The Divine Yes*, pp. 97-98.

take much to nurture my nine-year-old imagination. I thought I was following in the footsteps of the Great Mick! Most people know that Mickey Mantle was one of the all-time great switch hitters in baseball history. He was also a superb fielder. The major reason he moved from the outfield to the infield was due to his weakened knees and legs. He was always hurting himself by running down fly balls and crashing into the outfield wall. But even when the Yankees moved Mantle into first base he still played with great flair and hustle. I tried to stretch like he did when I had a ball thrown to me from one of the infielders. Even when the play wasn't close I'd stretch and roll over in the dirt. It was wonderful! At least I could look like a real baseball player!

We men are often critical of you ladies and your supposed preoccupation with detail and appearance. But you know that we are as guilty as you, if not more so. I love to go to Busch Stadium in St. Louis to see the Cardinals play. I grew up on Cardinal baseball. My family will testify that I like going early on game days. I don't want to miss anything. I love the hot dogs, the Cracker Jacks, the peanuts, the Cokes, but I really love batting practice and watching the players up close. I romanticize every detail. The uniforms, the hats, the wrist bands, the sunglasses, the way the players wear all their stuff, and the shoes, especially the shoes. Everything! My wife, Sue, thinks I have flipped out at times. She will tell you that I go off into the "unknown" when I enter the stadium.

I have been carried away by "the boys of summer" since my days with the Heyworth White Sox. Everybody on our Little League team had uniforms, caps, gloves and shoes, except me. I didn't have the baseball shoes. I had begged my dad for a pair of rubber spiked shoes with white stripes along the top. Dad needed to make a trip to neighboring Bloomington and I reminded him of my shoe size and my dream of having real baseball footwear. We both knew how much they cost. We had already priced them. $9.95. No question that was a lot of money for my family. Dad got home about two hours before game time. I couldn't wait to try on my new spikes! I tore open the box and there they were, black tennis shoes, not spikes. With three eyelets on each side they looked like something someone might wear who was going sailing for the day, but not to play baseball! I was devastated. I cried. I wish I could put into words the disappointment I felt.

I think my father understood in a strange sort of way, because he got angry. Sometimes parents camouflage their hurt behind anger. Dad said, "If you don't appreciate the shoes, I'll take them back to the store." So, I wore them. I intentionally put dirt on them. I didn't want anyone thinking they were new. I am ashamed of that now. It sounds so small as I write about it, but it was major league business to me then. I cried silently every time I wore those shoes. I hated them. It all seems so trivial now. What happened after that is even more unclear to me. I believe God gave me a gift. Somewhere during that season of baseball I started valuing what I had, not what I didn't have. How does a person explain that? It happened to Job too. God gave Job a gift after all of his pain that he would have never received without the pain. Have your experienced anything like that?

In Job 42:1-6 our man from Uz surrenders, not in defeat, but in realization that God is bigger than he is and truly in control. I am convinced that Job, at this point, is now able to receive three gifts from God. There may be more in the story, but I see at least three. These gifts are available to anyone who endures a season of suffering. Don't forget that the form of the narrative is Hebrew poetry, therefore ideas are often repeated and enlarged. Here is the first gift.

#1. Contentment.

> Then Job replied to the Lord: "I know that you can do all things; no plan of yours can be thwarted. . . . My ears had heard of you but now my eyes have seen you" (Job 42:2,5).

Job and God are again united with each other. The suffering man from Uz seems even happy in his pain. It sounds like he would rather suffer, if God willed it, than be in good health and prosperity. With childlike faith Job has learned contentment. To come to the realization that God has the whole universe in His hands, even one man's suffering, is to enter into a world of peace. This truly is a gift that only God can give. Contentment isn't something I get because I have or don't have. Contentment, biblical contentment, is based upon a relationship. Job says, "Now my eyes have seen you." He came to trust God. That's where contentment blooms and grows.

Don't miss that word "thwarted." We don't use it much in our contemporary culture. The various English translations of the Bible (N.A.S., R.S.V. and N.I.V.) all use the same word. The King James translates it "withholden." The word literally means "cut off." Sometimes it is used as a military term in the O.T. When the word is used in that sense it is translated "walled up" or "fenced up." Job is saying that nothing of all that God has planned for us can be walled up, withheld, or cut off. We can bask confidently in the knowledge that God has our best interests at heart. Whether the outlook is good or gloomy God is working for our good. It's a wonderful gift, but few people unwrap it after they have suffered. I want to save 42:3 for now. We'll come back to it in a moment. There is a second gift that I want to highlight.

#2. Humility.

Job has a confession to make. Read it.

> You said, "Listen now, and I will speak; I will question you, and you shall answer me." . . . Therefore [Now that I have really seen you, God] I despise myself and repent in dust and ashes (42:4,6).

Job isn't confessing some specific sin. He is acknowledging

124

his own limitations. Three in all are mentioned.

42:2 "I am weak and God is not."
42:3 "I am unwise and God is not."
42:6 "I am unworthy and God is not."

It is this gift of humility that Job unwraps and puts on. It is also this gift that opens up the possibility for Job to really know God. The word "despised" in 42:6 is helpful in understanding what Job is trying to say. Some translations use the word "abhor" or "retreat." This particular word could be translated "rejected." In all the places where "despised" is used, 73 in all, it is consistently used of people rejecting or despising God. Rarely is "despised" used in reference to people speaking of their own attitudes or words. This statement by Job is not a polite little apology. This is not a puny, "Sorry about that." Job's words drip with humility, even though he is a man who is blameless, upright, reverent toward God and pure in heart. He is still willing to unwrap the gift of humility because he sees God with his heart.

Few people think of humility as a gift, but it is. It is the very thing that opens up the possibility of knowing God. And even more than that humility opens the way for being used by God in a significant manner. Now and then I come across a cartoon that really discloses great insight. Several years back *Christianity Today* ran a small cartoon that showed a man alone, kneeling in prayer, hands folded before God. The caption read:

> Dear Lord, let me be the big cheese in the number-one job of the top outfit in the country, and let me come up with the right answers at the right times in the right places, but with it all, let me remain soft-spoken, country-shy, plain old Jeff Crotts from Spickard, Mo.[2]

Humility is a gift that comes on the tail of suffering, but very

---

[2]*Christianity Today*, September 18, 1987 Issue, p. 9.

few people recognize it as such. It is a treasured gift in the N.T. It doesn't have one ounce of weakness in it. Its synonym is not "wimp." Humility is a word that paints a picture of someone who is under control, considerate and kind. The word reveals a portrait of someone who, like the kids say, "Doesn't act too big, doesn't act too small, but just acts medium." In ancient Greece humility was used to describe a horse that was tame, yet with the ability to throw a rider and run like the wind. Suffering offers that kind of gift. It offers a quiet spirit, a confident demeanor, under the Holy Spirit's control. It is so desperately needed in the Kingdom. I know of people who have departed from a season of suffering in their life more arrogant, rude and obnoxious than they were prior to their suffering. This gift needs unwrapped. There is a third and final gift that I cannot explain.

#3. Wonder.

I could call it perspective, vision or seeing what God sees, but I chose the word "wonder." I picked this particular word because of what Job says in 42:3.

> You asked, "Who is this that obscures my counsel without knowledge?" Surely I spoke of things I did not understand, things too wonderful for me to know.

I like how David McKenna describes this verse.

> Wonder is the experiential response to the grace of God. Mystery, wonder, and grace are inseparable. . . . Adults tend to fear mystery but children find glee in the unknown. So when Job speaks of "things too wonderful for me," he is like a child reveling for a moment in the wonders of God.[3]

Job unwrapped this gift of wonder. Those people who have

---

[3]David McKenna, *Communicator's*, "Job," pp. 311-312.

been truly changed in their suffering are the ones who have been led by wonder into a deeper relationship with Jesus Christ, a fellow-sufferer. I knew a man who found out he had emphysema. Fifty percent of his lungs had become useless. After living an active, athletic life, his doctor said, "You have a crippling disease. The prognosis is not good." My friend told me that he went out to a nearby lake and sat and thought and cried for six and a half hours. When he returned home that evening he didn't tell his wife what he had found out that day. For an entire year he kept the awful secret to himself. "But over the past two years something I cannot explain has happened to me," he said. He wanted me to know that he had finally told his wife the news and somehow his burden felt lighter. He began to run off a long list of blessings he believed the Lord was now bringing into his life. Here are a few of them.

God is more real to me than ever.
I love my wife more than I ever did.
I hear birds and crickets the way I never did before.
Colors stand out to me.
The smell of food is a celebration for me.
I love getting up in the morning.

In order to begin each morning my friend had to spend fifteen minutes coughing in order to clear his lungs for the day's work. Sometimes he couldn't catch his breath. He took medicine three times a day, everyday, but he wanted me to know that his whole experience had brought wonder into his life. He said, "I now live life at a deeper level." How do you explain that? I buried my friend several years ago and I declare to you that his gusto for life only increased with each painful day.

What I have been describing for you is Job's experience. He grew in his wonder of God's ways. I came across a book a number of years ago, written back in 1962, that woke up a lot of people who slumber their lives away. The book is called

Silent Spring, written by Rachel Carson. She was a biologist who first articulated the adverse affects of pesticides on animals and people. Her work was highly acclaimed. A few years later she wrote a lesser known book, *A Sense Of Wonder*.

I tell you all of this because it is the second book that helped me to understand Job a bit more. In the book Carson introduces her young nephew, Rodger, to the wonders of creation. She began this introduction when Rodger was only twenty months old. Ms. Carson would take little Rodger out to the ocean and allow the spray of the waves to touch his face. She introduced him to the crab, shells, plants, the moon and rainy days along the coast of Maine. They took walks together through the woods, barefoot, while taking in the birds, rocks and bugs.

About midway through *A Sense of Wonder* Carson remarks how she is sure there is something much deeper, something lasting and significant in life. But she died before the book was completely finished, before, I believe, she realized that what she was seeking was a personal relationship with the Creator of the universe. She goes to great lengths in describing a child's world, one that is fresh and beautiful, packed full of wonder and joy. Carson believed that we lost our clear-eyed vision when we became adults. Something got dimmed in us along the way. Her great wish was that a "good fairy" would grant each of us a sense of wonder that was indestructible, that would last a lifetime.

Only God in heaven can sustain a lifetime of wonder. Suffering helps to keep it alive. Have you noticed? If the saga of Job ended right here this man had received three gifts that far outweighed his former prosperity and health. C.S. Lewis drove it home to me in *The Problem of Pain*.

> God gives the happiness that there is, not the happiness that is not. To be God — (or) to be like God and to share His goodness . . . (or) to be miserable — these are the only three

128

alternatives. If we will not learn to eat the only food that any possible universe ever can grow — then we must starve eternally.[4]

Here is the positive matter of suffering. No one is immune to pain. It is not that everything is Eden-like after we become Christians. I despise that kind of teaching. Rather, it is the uncompromising fact that now God gives us the "wherewithal" to walk wherever He leads us. He walks with us.

I cannot read Job 42:1-6 and not consider the Christmas story. When it comes to this story I love how it is told in the King James.

> And it came to pass in those days, that there went out a decree from Caesar Augustus, that all the world should be taxed (Luke 2:1).

After 400 years of silence, no word from God, there came this crushing blow. Rome called for a taxation of all people. Some governments come to the people to abuse them, other governments are so repressive that they make the people come to them.

> And Joseph also went up from Galilee, out of the city of Nazareth, into Judaea, unto the city of David, which is called Bethlehem . . . To be taxed with Mary his espoused wife (Luke 2:4-5).

And Mary was pregnant and already having contractions and riding a donkey from Nazareth to Bethlehem! 70 miles! Suffering. Silence. Taxes. Pregnant. No place to stay!

> And she brought forth her firstborn son, and wrapped him in swaddling clothes, and laid him in a manger; because there was no room for them in the inn (Luke 2:7).

---

[4]Lewis, *The Problem of Pain*, p. 54.

The Savior of the world was placed next to cows and donkeys and livestock in general. Does that sound easy? Yet, in this story of poverty and pain an angel speaks these words.

> Fear not: for, behold I bring you good tidings of great joy which shall be to all people. For unto you is born this day in the city of David a Saviour, which is Christ the Lord (Luke 2:10-11).

Good News! Amazing gifts travel alongside suffering. Why do these gifts only become apparent to most of us after suffering departs? Search your own heart. Consider your own journey. For the one who allows suffering also comes bearing gifts and He is seldom early, but never late. Ask Job.

CHAPTER TWELVE

Can We Live Happily Ever After?
Job 42:7-17

"If Satan opposes the new convert he opposes still more bitterly the Christian who is pressing on toward the higher life in Christ. The Spirit-filled life is not, as many suppose, a life of peace and quiet pleasure. It is likely to be something quite the opposite. Viewed one way it is a pilgrimage through a robber-infested forest; viewed another, it is a grim warfare with the devil. Always there is a struggle . . . ."[1]

The greatest piece of literature ever written on theme of suffering ends like this.

After the Lord said these things to Job (38-41), he said to Eliphaz the Temanite, "I am angry with you and your two friends, because you have not spoken of me what is right, as my servant Job has. So now take seven bulls and seven rams and go to my servant Job and sacrifice a burnt offering for yourselves. My servant Job will pray for you, and I will accept his prayer and not deal with you according to your folly. You have not spoken of me what is right, as my servant Job has." So Eliphaz the Temanite, Bildad the Shuhite and Zophar the Naamathite did what the Lord told them; and the Lord accepted Job's prayer. After Job had prayed for his friends, the Lord made him prosperous again and gave him twice as much as he had before. All his brothers and sisters and

---

[1]A.W. Tozer, *That Incredible Christian* (Camp Hill, PA: Christian Publications, 1986 reprint), p. 73.

131

everyone who had known him before came and ate with him in his house. They comforted and consoled him over all the trouble the Lord had brought upon him, and each one gave him a piece of silver and a gold ring. The Lord blessed the latter part of Job's life more than the first. He had fourteen thousand sheep, six thousand camels, a thousand yoke of oxen and a thousand donkeys. And he also had seven sons and three daughters. The first daughter he named Jemimah, the second Keziah and the third Keren-Happuch. Nowhere in all the land were there found women as beautiful as Job's daughters, and their father granted them an inheritance along with their brothers. After this, Job lived a hundred and forty years; he saw his children and their children to the fourth generation. And so he died, old and full of years.

So, once upon a time, a man from Uz lived happily ever after. For Job justice prevailed. It is a wonderful way to conclude a life-story. Job's three friends got a conversation with God out behind the woodshed. They took it well and all was forgiven and restored. Job got a double blessing of everything he had lost prior to his suffering. He got back his health, wealth and prosperity. The icing on the cake was the sound of children's voices laughing and playing in Job's house. It is significant to me that Job lost seven sons and three daughters and receives in return seven sons and three daughters. Everything is doubled, but his children. One cannot replace children, each is unique, a one of a kind deal.

I am also greatly interested in the way the writer of the story makes such a grand statement about the daughters of Job (42:14,15). These girls are absolute "knockouts." Their names fit a happy ending. First, there is Jemimah. Her name means "turtledove." A turtledove is a kind of dove that is small and has a sleek, elegant body. Maybe it was Jemimah's eyes that resembled a dove. We don't know. Can you picture her? She is petite, lovely, wholesome and godly.

Second, there is Keziah. Her names means "cinnamon."

In the O.T. cinnamon was an aromatic spice from the East Indies. Once you caught a scent of that fragrance you never forgot it. Keziah was unforgettable. Can you see her in your mind's eye? She would be as unforgettable as Cinderella was to Prince Charming.

The third daughter is Keren-Happuch. Her names literally means "horn of paint." I admit that the literal meaning doesn't translate too well, but its meaning is significant. The horn of paint was a reference to the small container Eastern women carried their cosmetics in. Her name is the principle cosmetic of oriental beauty. The Hebrew text seems to indicate that the third daughter was the most beautiful of all. Keren-Happuch had the pure, basic beauty that is so rare. When she put on her make-up her beauty was only enhanced. She was more than pretty, more than cute. This third daughter was stunningly beautiful.

Job 42:15 add the fairy tale touch, "Nowhere in all the land were there found women as beautiful as Job's daughters." The implication is clear. The phone rang off the wall at Job's house and a long line of eligible men kept coming around for visits! I suspect Job kept a good size club behind the front door. It is a happy ending! Notice that the daughters of Job even get an inheritance alongside their brothers, which the Law did not require. Job shares all that he has equally. Some Bible passages invite celebration and this is one of them. Festive, warm, full of joy, that is the ending to the story. And if you'll look at the first three words of the epilogue (42:7-9) you'll see what God thinks of spiritual arrogance. If you have ever been misrepresented, accused falsely or hurt by some-one's insensitive, razor-sharp words, then you know how wonderful it is to be vindicated and your critics silenced! It is truly party time at Job's house!

This is the kind of ending that a kid dreams about late at night. It's what all of us pray for. This ending is the kind of ending that we might share with our closest friend. We might whisper in their ear our fondest hope. We might say, "I want to get married and build a house at the edge of town near the bend in the road. Right there beside the creek. I'll buy a hundred acres from Mr. George. I think he'd sell it to me, don't you? We'll raise some cows and pigs and chickens. We'll farm some and I'll drive the school bus in the mornings and the afternoons. We'll go to church and raise our family properly. We'll have a wonderful life together." People long to love and be loved. Much of life resembles that for some folks, but much of life isn't like that at all.

Life would be great if it wasn't so real. Life is the place where we must make up our minds about God. Isn't that what Job did? When you move past the happy ending Job discovered life's purpose. The central focus of life is not a fairy tale ending but living under the sovereign Lordship of God through Jesus Christ. Our goal is to bring Him glory through all of our life's journey, both the good and the bad. So, my question is this, "How did Job do it?" How can a person make a good ending to their life even if cancer strikes, or they lose a child, or they are stripped of all their possessions, or they never see their life's dream fulfilled?

There is no question that Job has a happy ending, but not without some very difficult decisions being made. I would like to highlight two decisions Job made that gave his life the kind of ending that all of us want. Here's the first.

Decision #1. Will I forgive those who hurt me?

Please notice Job 42:10. "After Job had prayed for his friends, the Lord made him prosperous again and gave him twice as much as he had before." It was *after* Job prayed for his friends that the good ending came. Job's three friends had really hurt him. They said nasty, cutting, insulting and piercing things to Job, yet he forgives. Don't misunderstand. This is not a soft kind of forgiveness. This is not the kind of forgiveness that says, "Yes, I forgive you, but I never want to see your face again!" Remember that it wasn't only Job's three friends who had hurt him, but his own family apparently were less than comforting. Read again 42:11.

> All his brothers and sisters and everyone who had known him before came and ate with him in his house. They comforted and consoled him (here are the same two words we talked about in 2:11) over all the trouble the Lord had brought upon him and each one gave him a piece of silver and a gold ring.

Family and friends gathered to truly display their feelings and express their sorrow over Job's lonely suffering. They touched him, held him, kissed him, hugged him and cried with him. They also brought gifts. Perhaps this decision to forgive was the biggest test for Job of all. Could he forgive those who had hurt him deeply? Can I do that? I have noticed that I am incapable of praying for someone I cannot forgive. To pray for someone is to forgive them. Isn't that what Jesus meant? "You have heard people say, 'Love your neighbor and hate your enemy,' but I tell you: Love your enemies and *pray* for those who persecute you, that you may be sons of your Father in heaven" (Matt. 5:43-45). Job allows these very people who have hurt him to now come and minister to him. He forgives the hurt he never deserved. In N.T. terms that is radical discipleship!

Lewis Smedes wrote a great book, *Forgive and Forget,* in which he describes four steps we go through when we forgive.

1. We hurt. Job did that.
2. We hate. There are hints of this in the story.
3. We heal. This is obvious in the life of Job.
4. We come together. That is 42:11.

Here is how Smedes puts it.

> We cannot breathe back all the old life; we forgive and reunite on the terms that life and circumstances make

available to us. . . . We practice love's high art framed and fringed by the boundaries of time and place.[2]

To have a happy ending demands tough decisions. Tolstoy is a remarkable writer. I do not know his works as well as I would like. Most of us know that he wrote *War and Peace*, but he also wrote a lot of other things. One such work is called *Russian Stories and Legends*. One of those stories resembles Job.

An honest and hardworking Russian peasant named Aksenov left his dear wife and family for a few days to visit a nearby fair. He spent his first overnight at an inn during which a murder was committed. The murderer placed the murder weapon in the sleeping peasant's bag. The police discovered him that way in the morning. He was stuck in prison for twenty-six years, surviving on bitter hopes of revenge. One day the real murderer was imprisoned with him and soon charged with an escape attempt. He had been digging a tunnel that Aksenov alone had witnessed. The authorities interrogated the peasant about his crime granting him at long last his opportunity for revenge, for on the peasant's word his enemy would be flogged almost to death. Aksenov was asked to bear witness to the crime, but instead of jumping at the chance, the grace of God suddenly wells up in the peasant's heart, and he finds the darkness in him has fled, and he is filled with light. He finds himself saying to the officers, "I saw nothing." That night the guilty criminal makes his way to the peasant's bunk and, sobbing on his knees, begs his forgiveness. And again the light of Christ floods the peasant's heart. "God will forgive you," he said, "Maybe I am a hundred times worse than you." And at these words his heart grew light and the longing for home left him.[3]

---

[2]Lewis Smedes, *Forgive and Forget* (San Francisco: Harper and Row, 1984), pp. 36-37. I highly recommend the chapters on "Forgiving God" and "Forgiving Monsters."

[3]David Redding, *Amazed By Grace* (Old Tappan, NJ: Fleming H. Revell, 1986), pp. 33-34. I found this story while reading through Redding's book.

Will I forgive those who hurt me? How can there be a good ending to my life's story without this? Job seems to understand it all.

There is a second decision to be made and I think it was the toughest one for Job. I know this is the hardest one for me.

Decision #2. Will I let God be God?

Job 42 is packed full of this decision. The single, most profound thing about Job for me, in reading it as a Christian, is that suffering becomes for those who follow God the way He changes us into the likeness of His Son. However, if I am constantly questioning Him, always complaining, continually critical, I'm not letting God be God.

There is not one ounce of sin in saying to God, during a time of personal suffering, "Lord, I'm hurting. It just doesn't seem fair. I need you." There is, though, something terribly wrong in saying, "Lord, how could you let this happen to me? If you are God do something about it." The reason that the latter statement is so clearly incorrect is — God is doing something about it! He is changing us into His likeness. When Job finally said, "I know that you can do all things" (42:2a), he was on his way to allowing God to be God.

Some very practical questions leap out at me from this second decision Job faced. Consider these carefully.

1. Do I know Christ as my Savior?
   Every single person must come to the point where they agree with what God has said about them. Each of us is lost and eternally separated from God if we do not, by faith, come into a saving relationship with Jesus Christ.

2. Is God really Lord of my life?
   Job clearly learned what Lordship meant. Nothing teaches us more about God's supremacy than times of pain and suffering. When I relinquish control of my life, then, and truly then is He Lord.

137

3. Does the direction of my life reflect that I will live happily ever after, regardless of what particular crisis comes my way?

Think with me about James 5:11. Here is the only place in the entire N.T. where Job is mentioned.

> As you know, we consider blessed those who have persevered. You have heard of Job's perseverance and have seen what the Lord finally brought about. The Lord is full of compassion and mercy.

The word translated "perseverance" means "to stay on in the same place, to remain steady, to not give up under pressure, to abide under." This is the N.T.'s witness to the 42 chapters of Job's life. He let God be God. Job is not commended for his patience, but for his "stick-to-it-iveness."

Harold Shortridge lives in Philadelphia, Illinois. You won't find it on most maps. He lives with his mother, Marie. In August, 1957, Harold and a friend had just gotten their discharge from the military. They were traveling to Jacksonville, Illinois on Route 125. What happened to them occurred in a split second. A drunk driver veered across the highway killing Harold's friend and turning Harold into a quadriplegic.

You have heard this story a thousand times over. The drunk driver received only a scratch. For 28 years Harold has been imprisoned in a wheelchair and a bed in Philadelphia, Illinois. He asked me, when I visited him, about miracles and suffering and grace. I asked him about drunk drivers and forgiveness and Lordship. Have you ever been in a quadriplegic's home? Everything is open and wide. It has to be that way. I asked Marie, "How do you go on?" "It's Harold that helps me," she said. "What helps you, Harold?" I wondered. Without one hint of cynicism or bitterness he offered these words, "I just think about Jesus and that is enough." I said,

"I'll look forward to seeing you walk one day." "I'll look for you," he responded. We laughed and prayed. And I knew I had met one man who understood Job's decision.

Job ends well. "And so he died, old and full of years." I am a lover of books. Since the first grade when Mrs. Heyworth taught me how to read I have been in love with words, sentences, paragraphs, chapters and books. I keep a list of books I'm always trying to find. My mother-in-law helps me track them down. I keep a reading list too, but I especially like going back to the old devotional classics, stories of saints who ended their life well and I really love to read the Scriptures repeatedly. Not long ago I finished reading Genesis to Revelation again. On this occasion I read from an English translation that I had never used before just to stay fresh. I like stories that end well. I appreciate the way Bob Benson put it before cancer took his life.

> I like the Bible — because it ends well. It begins with the heros in a sinless, deathless land — but they tripped, fell, and got lost on a downward journey that led through sin, misery, failure, sorrow, war and shame. And finally you begin to think they are never going to make it back. But when it ends, they are home again — in a sinless, deathless land. It took God's Son to do it — but it ends well.[4]

Job and the rest of Scripture agree: suffering, pain and evil are realities in this life. God's promise still stands in all the confusion and chaos, "I am with you." What does it take to end our life's story well? It takes some perseverance, encapsulated in some faith, about the size of a mustard seed. The question of the moment is clear. Do you really believe that God in heaven, who came to earth in Jesus of Nazareth, cares about you? He has an unblemished record of seldom being early, but never being late. All of heaven awaits your answer.

---

[4]Bob Benson, *He Speaks Softly* (Waco: Word, 1985), pp. 165-166.

139

Conclusion

Somewhere on the journey to write this book I became ill. Anytime I can't get out of bed for two weeks is a sure sign that something is terribly wrong. I confess I don't make a very good patient. You can ask my wife and children about that. It is funny what comes into your mind when you are recovering from a sickness that is undiagnosed. You find yourself thinking about all kinds of things. "Is this all in my mind?" "How come other people don't seem to get sick?" Who's going to mow my yard?" "I wonder what it's like outside?" "If I die will my wife remember to set out the trash on Monday?" "Will I regain my strength?" "Does anybody really care?"

While reflecting on these thoughts and others, some of which I cannot put down on paper, I found myself thinking about palm trees. I returned from the Philippines in May and I have been to other tropical areas of the world, so I was meditating on palm trees. I know, I know, I was probably delirious. Somewhere I read that palm trees have amazing persevering strength. They can survive drought because the root of the palm is the same size as the stem and its base. They are equipped to gather nourishment from any resource available because their roots go deep into the ground. Palm trees can endure hurricane winds because they bow to the storms they encounter, while other trees break. These trees can withstand all kinds of abuse from man or bug. The life of the palm tree is not on the outside, but is located deep within the cover of the bark. It is a fact that the older the palm tree the sweeter the fruit. It doesn't even begin to bear fruit until it reaches the mature age of 50 years old. So, here I am thinking about palm trees and God.

I know that God can be trusted because of the death, burial and resurrection of Jesus. On the cross, our Lord cried out, "My God, My God, why have you forsaken me?" And God was there, suffering completely. If you ask me for an explanation I can't give you a very satisfying one. I, for one, could not believe in a God who would not suffer. The cross assures me that God's love is total. The cross is high ground. It gives me the vantage point from which I can see suffering clearly. The cross doesn't do away with suffering, but it certainly provides the correct view. The God of Scripture is an economist. He wastes nothing. When it comes to suffering our Father in heaven sometimes uses it to refine us (like a metalworker). Sometimes God uses suffering to discipline us (like a loving dad with his children). Sometimes God uses suffering to prune and shape us into His likeness (like a good gardener). I admit I have more questions than I do answers when it comes to suffering, but I long to be like a palm tree when adversity strikes. Dear reader, I am asking you to not waste your sorrows. Let your roots go deep into the life of God. He can be trusted.

In your English Bible the Psalms follow the book of Job. It interests me greatly to read the first Psalm in light of the story of Job. Listen to the description of a godly person. "He is like a tree planted by streams of water, which yields its fruit in season and whose leaf does not wither. Whatever he does prospers" (Ps. 1:3). In the hands of the Master Gardener suffering becomes a means of grace. This great Gardener is seldom early, but never late. That's how a good story should end. Amen. Come, Lord Jesus, come!

Bibliography

Alexander, John. *Practical Criticism: Giving It and Taking It.* Downers Grove: InterVarsity Press, 1976.

Bayly, Joe. *Psalms of My Life.* Wheaton: Tyndale House, 1969.

_____. *The View from a Hearse.* Elgin, IL: David C. Cook, 1973.

Benson, Bob. *He Speaks Softly.* Waco: Word, 1985.

Burton, Richard F. *Aladdin and His Wonderful Lamp.* New York: Random House, 1993.

Chambers, Oswald. *My Utmost for His Highest.* Reprint, Uhrichsville, OH: Barbour Books, 1991.

Copper, Leonard. *The Theological Wordbook of the Old Testament.* Vol. 2. Edited by R. L. Harris, G.L. Archer, and B.K. Waltke. Chicago: Moody Press, 1980.

Drummond, Robert. *Faith's Perplexities.* New York: American Tract Society, n.d.

Edwards, Gene. *A Tale of Three Kings.* Augusta, ME: Christian Books, 1982 reprint.

_____. *Letters to a Devastated Christian.* Reprint, Goleta, CA: Christian Books, 1983.

Fant, Clyde E. and William M. Pinson. *20 Centuries of Great Preaching.* Vol. 6. Reprint, Waco: Word, 1975.

Hybels, Bill. *Who You Are When No One's Looking.* Downers Grove: InterVarsity, 1987.

Jones, E. Stanley. *The Divine Yes.* Nashville: Abingdon, 1975.

Keil, C.F. and F. Delitzsch. *Commentary on the Old Testament.* Vol 4. Job. Translated by Francis Bolton. Reprint, Grand Rapids: Eerdmans, 1980.

Kipling, Rudyard. *A Selection of His Stories and Poems.* Edited by John Beechcroft. New York: Doubleday, 1956.

Kline, M.G. "Job." *Wycliffe Bible Commentary.* Chicago: Moody Press, 1962, p. 463.

Kushner, Harold. *When Bad Things Happen to Good People.* New York: Avon Books, 1981.

Lair, Jess. *Ain't I a Wonder and Ain't You a Wonder Too?* New York: Doubleday, 1977.

Lewis, C.S. *A Grief Observed.* New York: Bantam Books, 1961.

—————. *The Problem of Pain.* New York: MacMillan, 1962.

Lovett, C.S. *Dealing with the Devil.* Baldwin Park, CA: Personal Christianity, 1967.

McKenna, David L. *The Communicator's Commentary.* Vol. XII. Edited by Lloyd J. Ogilve. Waco: Word, 1986.

Nouwen, Henri. *The Genesee Diary.* Garden City, NY: Image Books, 1976.

Pratney, W.A. *The Nature and Character of God.* Minneapolis: Bethany House, 1988.

Redding, David. *Amazed by Grace.* Old Tappan, NJ: Fleming H. Revell, 1986.

Reichert, Victor E. *Job.* Edited by A Cohen. London: The Soncino Press, 1974.

Smedes, Lewis. *Forgive and Forget.* San Francisco: Harper and Row, 1984.

Swindoll, Charles. *The Grace Awakening.* Dallas: Word, 1990.

_____ . *Three Steps Forward Two Steps Back.* Nashville: Thomas Nelson, 1980.

Taylor, Hudson. *Hudson Taylor.* Men of Faith Series. Minneapolis: Bethany House, n.d.

Tozer, A.W. *That Incredible Christian.* Reprint, Camp Hill, PA: Christian Publications, 1986.

_____ . *The Knowledge of the Holy.* San Francisco: Harper and Row, 1961.

Twain, Mark. *The Adventures of Tom Sawyer.* Great Books for Children. Reprint, New York: Holt, Rinehart, and Winston, 1961.

White, Jerry and Mary. *Friends and Friendship.* Colorado Springs: NavPress, 1982.

Yancey, Phil. *Where Is God When It Hurts.* Grand Rapids: Zondervan, 1977.

ABOUT THE AUTHOR

J.K. Jones is professor of New Testament and Preaching at Ozark Christian College in Joplin, Missouri. He received his B.A. and M.A. (New Testament) from Lincoln Christian Seminary, Lincoln, Illinois and his M.A. (Pastoral Studies) from Friends University in Wichita, Kansas. He has ministered to several churches in Illinois: Windsor Road Christian Church, Champaign; Lake Fork Christian Church, Lake Fork; and Ashland Church of Christ, Ashland. Prior to his entering the ministry, he served as an Air Force Security Policeman. He is the author of the popular devotional book, *Longing for God: Cultivating Your Spiritual Garden*, also published by College Press Publishing. He and his talented and godly wife, Sue, are discipling two delightful girls, Chelsea and Lindsey.